ACCLAIM FOR JEFFREY WANDS AND
THE PSYCHIC IN YOU

"*The Psychic in You* is a lucid and memorable chronicle of the life and work of a medium, as perceived by the medium himself. I greatly enjoyed reading this fascinating book, which will be very useful to anyone who is trying to make sense of the baffling realm of psychic phenomena. *The Psychic in You* is an excellent source and introduction to study the human interface between this world and the spirit world."

—Raymond A. Moody, M.D., Ph.D., author of *Life After Life: The Investigation of a Phenomenon—Survival of Bodily Death*

"With compelling psychic stories, heartfelt meditations and visualizations, and great tips to develop your own abilities, *The Psychic in You* is a wonderful testament to the psychic's journey. An enjoyable and inspiring read. Jeffrey Wands is the real deal!"

—Stacey Wolf, author of *Psychic Living*

"*The Psychic in You* is an enlightening, entertaining, and inspiring introduction to the life and visions of a gifted psychic that reveals the keys for developing one's psychic ability. Definitely worth reading."

—Gary E. Schwartz, Ph.D., Director, Human Energy Systems Laboratory, University of Arizona, and author of *The Afterlife Experiments*

THE PSYCHIC IN YOU

UNDERSTAND AND HARNESS
YOUR NATURAL PSYCHIC POWER

JEFFREY A. WANDS
WITH TOM PHILBIN

POCKET BOOKS
New York London Toronto Sydney

POCKET BOOKS, a division of Simon & Schuster, Inc.
1230 Avenue of the Americas, New York, NY 10020

ISBN-13:978-0-7434-6995-1
ISBN-10: 0-7434-6995-X
ISBN-13:978-0-7434-7000-1 (Pbk)
ISBN-10: 0-7434-7000-1 (Pbk)

First Pocket Books trade paperback edition February 2005

20 19 18 17 16 15 14 13 12

Manufactured in the United States of America

To my wife, Dawn, who has always been a true inspiration and who has pushed me to achieve greatness with her love and support. To my sons Christopher and Robert who have taught me the meaning of life and fatherhood. To everyone who has ever lost a loved one, may they understand that there is an afterlife and there is truly life after death. To my grandparents Stewart and Lillian who were my rocks. To my aunts Carolyn, Helen, and Joan who helped me to understand my mission in life as well as the importance of my journey.

Thank you, all.

Acknowledgments

Special thanks to all my clients who shared their lives with me and who helped me realize the importance of this book's message. God bless Joanna in heaven, who encouraged me to broaden my audience through TV. I would like to thank my editor Brenda Copeland who has truly educated me, and her assistant Samantha Martin who helped out where angels feared to tread. To Tom Philbin who helped write this book. To Judith Curr, publisher of Atria books, a true publishing visionary. To Amy Rosenblum, of *The Maury Show,* and her great staff consisting of Paul Faulhaber, Marc Victor, and Joan Petrocelli, thank you for all your help. To Tracie Wilson and everyone at Universal TV, thank you. To Rob Miller, Mark, and Cindy of the *Breakfast Club,* the entire staff of WALK FM Radio and their listeners, thank you all. To my television agent Steve Sadicario, for all his help. Great big thanks to my friend Jimmy Decaro who has contributed his artistic talents to this book. Thanks to Shirley MacLaine, who went "Out on a Limb" and encouraged we all believe in a larger universe. Thanks are to the Higher Powers who bestowed this honored gift on me.

Love and Light,
JEFFREY A. WANDS

My thanks to Brenda Copeland for raising the editorial bar—and then making sure we got over it. Thanks also to my buddy Daniel Zitin for his insights and help. And, finally, profound gratitude for all those clients of Jeffrey who told their stories for the book, sometimes with tears in their eyes.

TOM PHILBIN

Contents

Preface

MEET JEFFREY WANDS

The first time I saw Jeffrey Wands in action was in December of 2001 when I went down to a television studio in Manhattan to attend a taping on *The Maury Show.* I was there as a possible collaborator with Wands on a book about his psychic powers.

I was skeptical. While I believe in an afterlife—I don't think it's logical not to believe—I nonetheless doubted that anyone could talk to the dead or see into the future with absolute certainty. But I was there to see what he could do and how he worked.

What follows is a mostly verbatim account of what happened.

Wands came out on the stage to a nice burst of applause and a couple of shouts from the 150 or so people in the audience. A trim, thirtyish, handsome man all dressed in black—shoes, suit, turtleneck. Wands looked nervous. I gathered this from the way he sat on a curved bench next to Maury: His body was still, his eyes a little too watchful.

I also looked closely at Maury—a tall, thin man with a shock of gray hair, also dressed in black—and tried to detect what he might be thinking, or doubting. Maury Povich had been around the talk show business a long time, and if anyone could spot something that wasn't kosher I figured he could. But I couldn't determine anything. Maury was smooth, melodiously articulate—and unreadable.

Based on what Jeffrey Wands was about to endure, nervousness seemed to me an appropriate state. *The Maury Show* producers had devised an acid test for him. And much more than his credibility was riding on how he performed.

As Maury explained:

"We have some grief-stricken guests waiting backstage who are desperate for Jeffrey to communicate with their deceased loved ones. Jeffrey has never met any of these guests and has no knowledge of their stories. Before we meet these guests we're going to escort Jeffrey backstage out of hearing range, then we're going to talk with our guests, and after they share their heartbreaking stories we're going to bring Jeffrey back out. Hopefully he'll be able to use his abilities to connect with their loved ones who have passed on."

Maury then led Jeffrey off the stage, after which he brought out the first guest, a pretty blonde woman with cornrow hair, wearing black slacks and a sweater and who, I guessed, was in her early twenties. Simultaneously, a large TV monitor on a back wall showed a photo of a goateed, smiling young black man.

"This is Angela," Maury said, "and if she looks sad it's because she is. Just three months ago, Alfie, the man you see in the photo, the love of her life and the father of her children, was murdered in cold blood outside her house. This is what happened."

Then, a dramatization, a blend of photos and video clips acted out by professional actors portrayed what had happened with Angela narrating.

"I was asleep in my bed," Angela said tearfully, "and I heard shots and I was scared. I saw that the clock said 2:40 and before it turned to 2:41 my doorbell rang three times. I got up and went downstairs and opened the door." She started to cry harder. "Alfie was lying there face down with blood coming out of his head. I didn't think he was dead . . . I couldn't bear to think of him as dead. But he was, and the hardest thing in the world is watching my children cry for him. . . ."

"So what do you want to ask Jeffrey?" Maury said. "How he died . . . why he died . . . ? "

"How, who, why . . . everything," Angela said.

"Okay," Maury said, "but before we bring Jeffrey out there's one other person who wants to know something about Alfie and that's his sister, Charlynn, who's in the studio audience."

Maury went into the audience and led a young black woman to the stage where she sat down next to Angela. Immediately, Charlynn, a heavyset person with large, expressive eyes reached over and grasped Angela's hand.

"And what do you want to know?" Maury asked.

"Why . . . how . . ."

Abruptly, she stopped and those expressive eyes got hard.

"I want to know," shc said, "who killed my brother."

"Okay," Maury said, "let's bring Jeffrey out."

From time to time as Maury went through these preliminaries, a camera would show Jeffrey alone in a room backstage, sitting on the edge of a couch, his face somber, occasionally rubbing his hands together. I was worried for him. He was definitely nervous.

The camera followed him coming out of the room and down a hall with a floor strewn with cable, and then out onto the stage to be greeted by solid applause and a few shouts. Now, for him to help these women and to succeed, I knew he had to do one thing: talk to the dead.

Maury introduced him to the women and he sat down next to them.

"Is there anything," Maury said to Jeffrey, "you need to ask?"

"No," he said speaking rapidly as, I was to discover, he almost always does, "let me just hear what I'm hearing."

"I have one, two, three figures standing here," he said. "I have an older male and younger male who is about thirty coming through and I have a grandmother standing behind Charlynn."

He paused, looked down at a pad, a pen poised over it.

"Now what's confusing me," he said, "about their coming through is that they're holding this young man back, so this is an unnatural passing. I get a feeling of . . . confusion."

He turned to Charlynn.

"And this is your brother?"

"Yes," she said.

"This was in the house?"

"No," Angela said.

"But right outside in front of the steps," Jeffrey said.

My mind flashed back to the dramatization, which had shown Alfie lying face down next to the front steps. And Angela had said that was where she found him.

Both women nodded. Yes.

"Now he's looking toward two people . . . he's showing me two people . . . like he's connected to them. Does this make sense?"

The women looked at him, saying nothing.

"Two people," Maury interjected, "who did what?"

Jeffrey did not respond to Maury, as if he didn't hear him, perhaps because he was too inwardly focused.

"This has to be unnatural," Jeffrey said, "because of the way he's bringing them across . . . I'm getting an explosive feeling . . . hit in the chest."

"What you're saying," Charlynn said, "he has seen two people?"

"Yes," Jeffrey said and appeared to be struggling to see the two figures more clearly. "He's looking at two people, and they're connected to it . . . and I see him looking directly at this one person. This is somebody he would have been around in the three-day period before."

Before, I thought, the murder. I had a sense that whatever Jeffrey saw coming in to him came in a receiver that was imperfect. Sounds and images seemed to ebb and flow, come in and out of focus.

"Now the red car is whose?"

"That's my car," Angela said.

Just like that he knows the color of the car. I was stunned, and I thought I heard someone in the audience gasp.

"Was he near the car?"

"He parked behind me," Angela said.

"Okay, because he's showing me the car."

Then:

"This is a neighborhood feeling I'm getting. I see him looking directly at the person who . . ."

Shot him I said to myself.

"Was he in the car, because he's showing me the car."

No answer.

"I'm getting a high feeling," Jeffrey said, "I got to believe that there was an addiction issue with him . . . or someone else."

Again, neither of the women responded. In fact, I realized that other than paying close attention to what Jeffrey was saying and occasionally becoming tearful, neither woman was very vocal. I wondered why.

"This" he said, "happened three, four months ago?"

"Three," Angela said, "going to be four."

"Wow," Maury's melodious voice chimed in, "he didn't know that!"

"I have to be honest with you," Jeffrey said to Angela, "before you he did not have a great relationship with women. You were the first person he connected with . . . a genuine love . . . he gives me the sense that he was finally getting his life together . . . that's how he's bringing it over . . .

"You found him?" he said to Angela.

"Yes."

Jeffrey stopped.

"There's a *K* name connected to this case," he said, "and he said you know who this is."

Abruptly, Charlynn gasped and bent over at the waist, hiding her face and sobbing uncontrollably. Angela started to cry too.

Jeffrey didn't push it. All he said was:

"You know what I'm talking about."

I thought they did: Jeffrey had told them who murdered Alfie.

The next guest, Christine, was a matronly blonde woman in her early forties who had suffered, as Maury accurately said, the "unthinkable" loss of two of her three children, Melissa, seven, and Jimmy, eleven, whose images showed on another monitor.

Then, the dramatization.

It was a blend of photos of Christine and her kids, alone or together, and interspersed with staged video clips of a fire, one part of which showed a child trying to get down stairs, flames blocking the way. Christine, narrating the dramatization, was near tears or crying throughout. She told of how she had gone to work and how when she got there, she was told to call home immediately. She reached her ex-husband who told her Missy was "all burned up" in a hospital and "Jimmy was dead."

The dramatization finished with Christine, tears rolling down her face, talking about how much she missed Melissa and Jimmy, and how no day went by without her thinking of them.

"And what," Maury asked, "do you want Jeffrey to do for you?"

"I just want to tell them how sorry I am that I couldn't be there to save them. I want to say good-bye to Jimmy. I never had a chance to say good-bye to him. They wouldn't let me go near him. I know I can't have them back. But I want to hold them in my arms just one more time."

You could hear a pin drop in that 150-person audience, except for the sounds of people sniffling. I had tears running down my face and I had to swallow repeatedly to avoid breaking into open sobbing.

"Okay," Maury said, "let's bring Jeffrey out."

The camera picked him up coming down that hall again, suit jacket open, and I had an insight, a flash of gooseflesh. Maybe he was nervous, maybe he wasn't. But there was something heroic about him. It was his willingness to directly confront this woman's pain—and help her deal with it. It was what psychics do—or try to do.

As he came onto the stage the audience, recognizing that he had done something important for Angela and Charlynn, exploded in applause and shouts.

He shook hands with Christine and then he and Maury sat down.

"I got a female figure standing here," Jeffrey said. "Her name is Nana. She's making me feel like this is a granddaughter."

He stopped.

"Now let me get this," he said to himself, "I had it and I lost it . . .

"Oh," he continued, "what's the significance of the *P* reference . . . Pat . . . Patsy . . ."

"Pumpkin," Christine said.

"This is connected to your daughter?"

"Yes, I used to call her that."

"Now Lisa, or Lessie is who?"

"My daughter, Melissa."

My God, out of an infinity of possible names.

"Your grandmother is making me feel they're together. That's how they are bringing it across. The only thing that's confusing me is that she's making it seem unnatural . . . a suffocation feeling."

"Yes . . . yes," Christine said, her face contorted.

"But there's a lot of confusion, chaos with this . . . I'm running from one location to another. Does this make sense to you?"

"Yes!"

"Okay . . . now . . ." He stopped and dropped his head again. Then:

"Strangulation feeling in your daughter."

"She couldn't breathe! She was on a ventilator."

"Okay. That's why I can't get a breath. But she knew you were there. She's very adamant about knowing you were there . . . very adamant. It's almost as if she waited before she went because that's how she brings it across."

He paused.

"But the brother is who?"

Christine cried harder.

"Her brother," she said.

"But," he said, "is there a third child? They're making me feel there's a third child."

Christine shook her head. She looked totally puzzled.

"No," she said.

"There wasn't any pregnancy lost? She's making me feel like there's another brother with them."

Then, realization came into Christine's eyes.

"Years ago . . ."

"Yes," Jeffrey said, "this is how she's bringing it over . . . so they're all together . . ."

Christine's sobbing was audible. But part of her tears now seemed to be happy ones. Then following no logical progression . . .

"She's making it seem," Jeffrey said, "like I'm falling down stairs."

"She was trying," Christine said, "to go down the stairs but she couldn't."

"She doesn't want you to be angry at her," Jeffrey said.

"I'm not angry."

"But she's very concerned because that's the way she brings it across."

"Okay."

"The November connection is what?" Jeffrey said.

"She was born November fifth."

"Now you sing," he said. "Or she sings. Because she's making fun of singing."

Christine smiled through her tears.

"We used to sing together."

"She said she had the better voice."

"Oh my God," Christine said smiling. "She said that to me once in the living room!"

"You need to know," he said, "that she's blaming herself. But the important thing is that we have both grandmothers here. This is not something you could have prevented."

"Is there anything else you want to ask him?" Maury said.

"I want . . . to say good-bye to Jimmy."

"Oh no, believe me," Jeffrey said, "they're both together. You got a lot of busybodies on that side. Which means you have a lot of relatives. What you didn't finish on this side, they're finishing on that side."

"Thank you."

"Is Jeffrey giving you some comfort?" Maury asked.

"Oh yes. Yes, he is."

For me he was too.

The final guest that day was a pale-faced twenty-year-old woman named Tisha whose father, Maury said, had been brutally murdered fifteen years earlier, when he was only thirty-five. "The mystery of her father's death still haunts her," he said, "and her desire to put all this to rest is even stronger now because she herself suffers from a fatal lung disease and could die at any time."

The dramatization came on, this time with Maury narrating. As he spoke, photos and professionally staged video clips depicted the action, telling of how her father, a handsome man with black hair and an engaging smile, was hitchhiking on his way home when he was assaulted and stabbed thirty-six times. The video showed a bloody butcher knife in simulated action, and then his body lying face down on ground that was blanketed with leaves.

One photo in the dramatization showed the entire family that had been "destroyed" by the murder, while another showed the man's mother who had died three years earlier, her dying wish that someone find out who had killed her son.

"Why do you want to contact your father now?" Maury said to Tisha when the dramatization was over.

"I grew up without my father," Tisha said. "Someone took him away from me and I want to know why. Why did they do it?"

Then Maury said, "Let's bring Jeffrey out."

The camera followed Jeffrey out of the backstage room and as he walked down the hall I got the feeling that I was watching a rock star approach. Indeed, when he came out on stage he was greeted with loud shouts and sustained applause.

He shook hands with Tisha and sat down.

"I have a young man in front of me and he's with his father but they're making me feel as if there's a distance between them, something that they did not resolve before they went over."

"That's my father," Tisha said, "and my grandpa. They weren't close . . ."

"So Michael is who?"

"My father *and* my grandpa."

"Wow," Maury said. "Wow. Right off the bat."

All I could do was blink.

"The March connection is what?" Jeffrey asked.

"My grandma's birthday."

"And grandma's passed?"

"Yes."

"You've got a lot of dead people here."

"Now the Fran. Or Frances . . ."

"That's my aunt."

"And she's passed?"

"I believe so."

"That's who your father's with."

Tisha nodded.

"And there's a Je name . . . like Jersey . . ."

Tisha looked puzzled.

Jeffrey started to move on to something else when Tisha realized something that brought tears to her eyes and a smile.

"Oh, Jean! My grandmother's name was Jean!"

"That's okay. The way they come across is the way they put it.

"Now," Jeffrey said, "the picture that was put in with him. He's showing me a picture in a pocket and a note you put in with it."

"Yes I did."

"Now," Maury said, "this is getting scary."

"That's his way," Jeffrey said, "of validating that it's him."

He paused.

"The only confusion I have here," he said, "is that he's making me feel an accident. It's unnatural."

"He was murdered," Tisha said.

"He's coming through that way. The connection with the impact is related . . ."

"He was injured in the head," Tisha said.

"That was the first impact. They hit him from behind. I'm also in the stomach area."

Tisha nodded.

"He was stabbed to death."

"This," Jeffrey said, "is like a robbery connection. He was in the wrong place at the wrong time."

Jeffrey paused.

"Who's TR?"

"His sister Terry."

"That's who he keeps making reference to . . ."

Pause.

"This was A.M.," Jeffrey said, "the middle of the night. I'm coming back from somewhere. Between four forty and four forty-eight . . ."

"Yes, that is when people said they heard screams."

"This is definitely robbery . . . and men in a van followed him. He's like leaving a local place. I'm getting a feeling of him walking along a road. The side of the road."

"He was hitchhiking."

He paused again.

"Yes, but . . . you need to tell Terry that he's okay. He's very concerned."

"Thank you."

"You're welcome."

And I realized that not only Terry would know he was okay, but so would Tisha.

Looking back, I realize that the core of Jeffrey Wands is the same as the core of this book. The desire to help people and in the book's case help you tap into your own psychic side, which can lead to some wonderful benefits, including helping you to better avoid danger, make better business and romantic decisions, put yourself in closer contact with yourself spiritually, and let you connect with those who have crossed over. By itself the latter is, as it were, worth the price of admission. Think about it. How wonderful would it be to talk one more time with lost loved ones, to put your arms around them and tell them the things you didn't say before they left? Wow.

As for me, I left my skepticism somewhere back there between the first and second guest, and I'm happy and proud to help in any way I can.

—Tom Philbin

ONE

We're All Psychic

SOUL ENERGY

When I was around seven years old I lived in a garden apartment with my mother in Islip, a town on the south shore of Long Island about fifty miles from New York City. I was a normal kid in every way. I fished for catfish at a local lake. I read comic books. I played baseball every chance I got, just one of many young Mets fans who wished he was Tom Seaver. And I also loved to watch a neighbor who I only knew as "Tony" work on his car, a candy-apple red GTO he kept in showroom condition. Tony used one kind of polish for the bodywork, chrome polish for the chrome sections, a toothbrush and Q-tip to get at narrow spots on the grille, and he even cleaned the engine—which always looked brand new—with a rag and some sort of special solution. I remember my mother watching Tony one day through our kitchen window, saying: "I hope that man never has to make a choice between his car and his wife. She'll be looking for a new husband."

Tony loved that car with an unholy passion, and my mom and I both knew that anyone who messed with it would have problems. Big problems. Tony was a tough looking guy with a shaved head (this was in the sixties when no one but the toughest of the tough would dare shave his head), and he had muscles on muscles. Tony was young and strong. He wore nothing but form-fitting black T-shirts and tight black pants. He looked like he could kill you with his bare hands.

One Saturday in late May I spotted Tony polishing his car, as usual. So I left my house to go and talk with him, also as usual. Or so I thought . . . until walking toward his house I was struck by a strange and fleeting thought, a weird feeling that something had happened to his car. I don't know where this thought came from—and certainly I didn't know how to explain it—the only thing I can say is that it was sharp and sudden and seemed to leave my mind as quickly as it entered. I was a little unnerved by the experience, but even as a kid I knew I probably shouldn't tell Tony. I knew he wouldn't like it. Not at all. Easier said than done, though. I was seven years old and painfully direct.

"Hey, Tony," I said, "is your car okay?"

Tony was standing on the opposite side of the car, polishing the hood. When he heard my question he stopped what he was doing and looked straight at me, his dark eyes hostile. My stomach did a freefall. I was sorry I had said anything, but I couldn't change it now.

"What do you mean?"

"I don't know. I just thought something might be wrong with your car."

"Why do you say that?"

"I don't know," I said. And, of course, I didn't.

That was a tense moment. Real tense. Then, slowly, Tony took one long last baleful look at me and went back to polishing his car. I watched him for a little while longer, then turned away and left without him saying his characteristic "See ya kid."

The next day when I got up I had the same thought as before, that something was wrong with Tony's car. So the first thing I did was to look out the window toward Tony's driveway and . . . it was gone! Tony's driveway was empty and his beautiful candy-apple red GTO was gone.

Where was it?

I spent some time during breakfast worrying about the car, but after a while I did what most kids did and switched my thoughts to something else—baseball. I forgot about the car altogether, then a little while later left my house, glove and ball in hand, to meet some friends and play at being a Met. I didn't get ten feet from my house when I saw Tony's door open. Somewhere deep inside me an alarm bell went off. I was scared. When I saw Tony walking my way, waving me toward him, I knew my fear was justified. He was mad. Real mad.

"Where's your car?" I asked.

"I have a problem with the tranny," he said, looking at me carefully. I nodded as if I knew what he meant, but I didn't. I didn't know a tranny from a fanny.

"Let me ask you something," he said.

"Sure," I said chirpily, trying to hide my fear.

"Did you do anything to my car?"

"What do you mean?"

"Put something in it that doesn't belong?"

Stunned, I shook my head vigorously. Tony looked at me as if evaluating a virus under a slide, then turned and walked away. I made it to the ball field as fast as I could.

Every day for the next few days I looked out the window to see whether the car was back. Before I left my house I looked across at Tony's to see if he was around, and only then would I leave my house. Thankfully, he didn't show.

The car reappeared during the week, but next Saturday when I saw Tony begin his polishing ritual I stayed inside the house. I knew we were finished, and we were. To this day I'm sure that he thinks I sabotaged his car.

I didn't know it then, but that was the very first time I had used my psychic ability, the very first time in my life when I "just knew." I didn't have any help from so-called logic or conscious thought. I wasn't told anything about it. I didn't see or hear a thing. I just knew.

What happened between Tony and me is common to all psychic experience. I was able to get special information without really thinking about it, at least initially. This information is special because although it may come from the present, it might just as easily be transmitted from the past or the future. It's also special because we wouldn't be able to obtain it without using psychic ability.

All psychic information comes from energy.

So where does this information come from? It comes from energy, the sort of energy that all human beings—living or dead—

give off. You might call it soul energy. Soul energy is both positive and negative, yin and yang, and it is transmitted back and forth between the living and the living, and the living and the dead. Places and inanimate objects contain psychic energy too.

Soul energy contains all kinds of information about the past, present, and future. Our other senses can't perceive this energy, but it can be picked up by our "sixth sense," which is a physical capacity like sight or smell, located somewhere in the vast and as yet unexplored (some scientists say 95 percent) part of our brain. To put it another way, the capacity is like a radio receiver that picks up radio waves and decodes it for us to use.

We're all psychic, because we all have that sixth sense.

CONSCIOUS INFLUENCE

Psychic energy comes to us along different paths, consciously and unconsciously. The energy that yields information that we're consciously aware of goes under various names, such as "intuition," "ESP" (extra sensory perception), and "psi" (psychic phenomena). We have a feeling about something, a sense, an idea that something is true or is going to occur. And it does.

It's this aspect of being psychic that most people think is the whole ball of wax, psychically speaking that is. But it's only one of the many ways in which we psychically perceive. There's a whole grab bag of psychic happenings that should be included in the category of conscious psychic information, psychic events that occur on a conscious level.

What I'm talking about can be clearly seen in what happened to my cousin Jennifer Johnson last summer. Jennifer was traveling in upstate New York with her two boys, John ten, and Mark eleven, when they started to yowl about not having any ice cream.

Have you ever thought about someone you haven't spoken to in a while—and then received a call from that very person? Well, what has happened is that by thinking about that someone else you have sent out energy that somehow connects with the other person, prompting a call.

Kids! Jennifer decided to give in and started to look for a place where they could stop for a cone. She saw a sign for a place called Saugerties and followed the road into town. Just before she got into Saugerties proper, Jennifer thought of her obstetrician, Dr. Raymond Fierstein. That was odd. Jennifer had not thought of Dr. Fierstein since John was born, ten years earlier. She knew she wouldn't likely be seeing him again on a professional basis. How strange that he should pop into her mind like that!

Jennifer drove slowly down the street into Saugerties until she spotted what looked like an old country store. She parked the car and went inside, the boys trailing after her. The place had a wide-board creaky floor and a tin ceiling from which hung a slowly revolving fan. The shelves were packed with all sorts of items, many of which appeared to be lightly coated with dust. This quaint little place seemed straight out of some old movie. It even had a big old counter at the back. Jennifer liked the store. She was glad she stopped. Taking her time to admire some of the dusty old canned goods, she started toward the back of the store hoping to find an ice cream freezer. But it was Jennifer who froze in her tracks. There, standing before her, was a small balding man wearing shorts and a flowery shirt and holding a pistachio ice cream cone. It was Dr. Fierstein.

"I was just thinking about you," he said, obviously flummoxed.

"I was just thinking about you!" Jennifer responded. "How about that?"

Coincidence, right? Wrong. It was psychic energy that drew Jennifer and Dr. Fierstein together, an invisible and imperceptible signal that each sent out to the other. In some ways it reminds me of that great line that Humphrey Bogart utters to Ingrid Bergman in *Casablanca*: "Of all the gin joints in all the towns in all the world, she walks into mine." I don't know exactly how people's energies connect, but I do know that they do, and I do know that there's always a "why."

A few weeks after Jennifer met Dr. Fierstein she was talking to a friend who was looking to find a good fertility doctor. Jennifer didn't know anyone, but she contacted Dr. Fierstein and he gave her an excellent referral to pass along to her friend, who ultimately became pregnant. That, I believe, is why Jennifer really met the doctor. Of course, one could say that she would have recommended him anyway, but people we haven't seen in a while tend to fade from mind, and she might have recommended someone else, possibly with a less desirable result.

It's not just people who emit psychic energy. Places do too, and we pick up on that energy through our sixth sense. That's what happened to a friend of mine named Jim Dwyer as he drove up from Arizona to New York a while ago. That drive is filled with endlessly

---

I don't believe in coincidence. I believe there is an invisible road map for souls, and when they contact each other because of a psychic impetus there is a reason for it—sometimes obvious, sometimes not so obvious. Think really hard about why something occurred and you can usually think of the reason behind it.

---

boring signs announcing innumerable small towns, the names of which are forgotten right after reading them. Crossing over into Maryland, Jim's eyes glazed over the signs until he saw a very ordinary signpost announcing what seemed like the very small town of La Plata. Jim's eyes opened wide. He felt a charge, a sense that somehow this place was important. Jim couldn't see the town—it was two or three miles down a side road. The only thing visible was the lonely green-and-white sign. He thought about it. He tried to articulate what it was he was feeling, but all he could isolate was the physical feeling of getting ill.

Why should a little town in the middle of nowhere seem so very important?

Jim kept thinking about La Plata even after he got to his home in New York, and he continued to think about it until about a week later when he heard some shocking news: A 20-foot-wide tornado had ripped La Plata apart.

Why was Jim so obsessed with the little town that was to suffer this devastating tragedy? In truth, I don't know. I wish I had the answer. All I know is that Jim's sixth sense picked up this free-floating psychic energy that La Plata was giving off. Someday the reason may emerge, but it hasn't yet. I have some ideas of course. Maybe someone will show up with a name that sounds like La Plata, and that someone is to be avoided since the name is associated with a bad event. Or maybe Jim will meet someone with a similar name, and that will alert him to a potential problem that he'll be able to help avoid.

UNCONSCIOUS INFLUENCE

Sometimes psychic energy flows into our unconscious mind and motivates us to do something unusual or out of character, and the only way we can tell that it has paid us a visit is a post-event analysis. Consider, for example, what happened to a client of mine, John Barzac.

If someone asked me to compile a Top 10 list of the neatest, best dressed people I've ever met in my life, John would certainly make the list. John always looked like he stepped from the pages of *GQ* magazine. His clothing was not only beautifully pressed, but impeccably coordinated and fitted. John himself was also impeccably predictable in his life and in his job, which was as a manager of a brokerage house ensconced in a building across the street from the World Trade Center.

September 11 had started for John, who lives in a brownstone in Brooklyn, like every other day. He got up, shaved and showered at his regular time, ate a low-cholesterol breakfast as he always did, and then donned his duds, which he had laid out the night before. His entire morning regimen was geared to being on time for

The more we come to understand the universe, the less it looks like a great machine, and the more it looks like a great thought.

—Sir James Jeans

work and his record was astonishing. He had not been late—or absent—once in thirteen years. But this day was bizarre. For the first time in thirteen years John couldn't find his keys. He always put his keys on his dresser—specifically the left side—so he was as puzzled as he was annoyed. *Where were those keys?* John searched unsuccessfully for ten minutes by himself and then, frustrated, enlisted the aid of his wife who had just gotten out of bed. When together they still couldn't find the keys, they got their two daughters to help. It took this little search party another ten minutes to find the keys . . . inside a slipper in the closet.

"I have no idea how they got there, "John told me. "But let me tell you, I was fuming."

As a result of the misplaced keys, John was twenty minutes late for work. Thank God. Chances are if he had been on time he would have been walking across the street from the World Trade Center at 8:45 A.M. just as the first terrorist plane slammed into the north tower, raining fire and debris down on top of him. There's not much doubt in my mind that John would likely have been killed if the search for his keys had not triggered a different scenario, making him late for work for the first time in thirteen years. When that flaming debris came down in the street at 8:45, John was standing on a Manhattan-bound train well out of harm's way.

"Being late saved my life," he said.

What saved John's life was actually psychic energy. This energy—perhaps transmitted by a dead relative or a living relative or even someone outside his family—had directed John's unconscious mind to put the keys in a place where he would have trouble finding them so that his life would be saved. Why he was designated to live to "play another day," as they say, I don't know. But somewhere, far down the line, the reason may become evident.

Some people, of course, would call this a lucky coincidence, but I've analyzed literally hundreds of these coincidences—events where people do things totally out of keeping with their characters—and I believe that they can only be explained by psychic energy.

Auras

Unconscious energy can change our habits and our moods, and it can also change our psychic appearance, which is what an aura is.

One day a few years ago a news anchor for CBS television—let's call her Linda—came to see me in my Flushing office. She was, as anchors are wont to be, a beautiful woman: smart, articulate, and bold too. But she had some issues. And she wanted my help.

Linda sat down in a chair across the desk from me and just as I was about to start telling her some things about herself, which I always do in a reading to help establish my credibility, she surprised me by reaching into her bag and handing me a small color picture.

"Who's this?" she challenged.

I scrutinized the picture. The woman appeared to be in her late sixties. She had gray hair pulled back and parted in the middle. Her features were heavy. Eastern European, I thought. Perhaps Slavic.

"She's your mother," I said, "but not your birth mother. You were adopted."

Linda blinked a few times.

"That's right."

I started to hand the picture back to her when, abruptly, I felt a sharp pain in my stomach. I pulled the picture back and looked at it again. An aura of black, circular light had formed over Linda's mother's stomach. Alarm bells went off inside but, as always, I made my advice as gentle as I could.

"I don't mean to alarm you," I said, "but your mother has a medical thing going on in her stomach that needs immediate attention."

"Right now?"

"Right now," I said softly.

We terminated the session. The next evening I was in my office about nine when the phone rang. It was Linda, and she was gushing with thanks.

"I want to thank you so much, Jeffrey," she said. "The doctor said that my mom had an aneurysm in her stomach which was about to burst. But they got it in time and she's going to be okay now. You saved her life."

No I didn't, Linda, I thought. The aura did.

Auras are colored lights that react to moods and also to people and places. Sometimes they appear as clusters on the body, sometimes

When you see an aura you are seeing soul energy in light form. You are seeing a person's soul.

as halos around the head or the entire body, and sometimes both. Auras are great because they can give anyone who picks them up a quick read of a person.

Auras don't appear to everyone. Like other forms of psychic energy, you have to be aware of them before you can read them. Everyone has an aura, but you won't be able to see it until your psychic eyesight is ready to receive it. As you develop your psychic abilities you will find that reading auras comes naturally—that's how it should be. Don't try to force an aura to come to you. It won't. In fact, if you try too hard to read someone's aura then chances are you'll conjure up something that isn't there. Relax. Don't "over-focus." You can't stare an aura into existence. Just be aware. Be receptive. Let go and be ready to receive the colors.

The key to extracting information from auras is understanding what the colors symbolize. When I saw the black light on Linda's mother's stomach, I became alarmed because black or gray light means a health issue. Red usually denotes a creative person, green is an indication that someone is searching for answers, blue indicates sadness or grief, and yellow means that there is a positive development in the offing.

Auras are not static. The colors can change on a particular person. For example, a person may have a white aura (indicating pos-

AURA COLOR	INDICATES
Red	passion dedication possible obsessive compulsive disorder
White	honesty integrity virtue
Blue	spiritual holy enlightened
Green (pale)	artistic creativity
Gray	negativity death mental health issues health problems
Black	death major health problems
Yellow	spiritually in need lacking direction
Gold	spiritually enlightened high consciousness
Violet	psychic abilities very intuitive

itive personality traits) which may then change to gray—indicating illness. Or it may change to some other downbeat or upbeat color because of a change in emotional state. The change can occur over a long period of time or quickly.

About six months ago, for example, I saw a client named Rita, and I immediately saw a maroon aura over her stomach area. Maroon is usually a fertility issue.

Rita confirmed what I saw: "I'm afraid I'm not going to get pregnant," she said. "I've been trying for a couple of years without success."

I said nothing because I saw nothing but then, near the end of the session (just a half hour later!) I saw something very exciting: The maroon aura over her stomach was changing to pink, and to me that meant one thing.

"You have a pink aura, Rita. And you know what that means?"

"No."

"You're going to become pregnant and have a baby girl."

She was thrilled, but even more thrilled when she called me a few weeks later and told me she was pregnant . . . with a baby girl.

Dreams

Even the most reluctant among us seem to be willing to admit the presence of some psychic element in our dreams. We imbue our dreams with meaning, sometimes spending hours to decode their meaning. Dreams can be powerful because in an unconscious state we are more receptive to psychic energy. Our defenses are down and we're not so resistant to picking up information from those who have passed.

It's not difficult to determine when a dream is psychic in nature and when it's not. There are signs. Psychic dreams are vivid or contain unusual colors. They may also have a special impact on the dreamer who somehow knows instinctively that the dream is extraordinary. Psychic dreams normally occur soon after someone crosses over, but they can occur before an event to give us a premonition. As one of my clients pithily put it: "No way are some of my dreams ordinary."

Dreams are endless in their number and in their meaning. So much of what we dream can only be interpreted when it's put in context, when it's analyzed in the larger meaning of experience and emotion. That said, there are some constants, some key symbols that are useful in unlocking the door to our dreams. Here are a few to get you going:

SYMBOL	MEANING
angel	success in love a visitation in the house prosperity
bell, ringing	quarrel in the family
coffin	success in love the coffin of a family member may mean serious health issues
teeth gold teeth extracting teeth toothache	major health problems dishonor and corruption good fortune health and happiness
train, locomotive	good business
wine	prosperity
water dirty water	abundance sickness, bad tidings
heavy fog fog clearing	bad business love is coming your way
death many deaths	spiritual awareness or awakening great happiness
storm, stormy weather	great problems in business
snow snow on a mountaintop	abundance big money coming shortly
lights	inheritance a new beginning

Make no mistake about it. Dreams have the potential to tap into an amazing amount of psychic energy.

One of the most famous psychic dreams ever was experienced by none other than President Abraham Lincoln. On April 11, 1865, Lincoln related the details of a disturbing dream he had to a group of friends. One of them was Ward Hill Lamon, author of *Recollections of Abraham Lincoln 1847–1865*, who reported what Lincoln said in his book.

Lincoln first told the assemblage of people that he had had the dream a few days earlier, that on that day

> "I retired very late. I had been up waiting for important dispatches from the front. I could not have been long in bed when I fell into a slumber, for I was weary. I soon began to dream. There seemed to be a death-like stillness about me. Then I heard subdued sobs, as if a number of people were weeping. I thought I left my bed and wandered downstairs. There the silence was broken by the same pitiful sobbing, but the mourners were invisible. I went from room to room; no living person was in sight, but the same mournful sounds of distress met me as I passed along. I saw light in all the rooms; every object was familiar to me; but where were all the people who were grieving as if their hearts would break? I was puzzled and alarmed.

> What could be the meaning of all this? Determined to find the cause of a state of things so mysterious and so shocking, I kept on until I arrived at the East room, which I entered. There I met with a sickening surprise. Before me was a catafalque, on which rested a corpse wrapped in funeral vestments. Around it were stationed soldiers who were acting as guards; and there was a throng of people, gazing mournfully upon the corpse, whose face was covered, others weeping pitifully. "Who is dead in the White House?" I demanded of one of the soldiers. "The President," was his answer, "he was killed by an assassin." Then came a loud burst of grief from the crowd, which woke me from my dream. I slept no more that night; and although it was only a dream, I have been strangely annoyed by it ever since.

Three days later, April 14, John Wilkes Booth, a Confederate zealot, sneaked up behind Lincoln and shot him in the head while he was watching a play at the now infamous Ford's Theater. Lincoln lingered until the next morning, when he died. His dream had been a premonition of his own murder.

Lincoln's reaction to the dream shows that he knew his dream was special. How many people tell their dreams to a group of people? He was afraid, afraid enough to tell friends of the dream's content. Lincoln was not unfamiliar with psychic phenomena. His wife, Mary Todd Lincoln, was heavily dependent on psychics and, in fact, used them to try to contact two young sons who had crossed over because of disease. Lincoln had to know it was special, psychic.

To me, also, there is further evidence of its psychic nature because of its apparently coincidental nature. To me coincidence, rather than meaning something is happening by chance, is a clear clue that psychic forces are at work.

Dreams are sent by God.

—Homer

Peggy Klein, a client of mine from Hicksville, New York, had a series of remarkable dreams that have all the earmarks of being psychic.

On December 29, 2000, Peggy suffered the ultimate loss any parent can have: Her twenty-year-old son Robert crossed over as the result of an automobile accident. As Peggy was to learn, Robert and his girlfriend June were in a KIA—"a scooter with a roof," Peggy calls it—and were making a turn on Hempstead Turnpike on Long Island when a drunk driver in a Jeep coming the other way barreled through a red light at high speed and smashed into the passenger side of the small vehicle where Robert was sitting. That impact was so forceful that Robert had to be cut from the car by firemen. "He was rushed to the hospital," Peggy says, "but his injuries were just too severe and he died after about six hours."

Peggy's first dream actually took place a month before the accident. "In the dream," she said, "I saw his girlfriend June on a phone, and she was calling me hysterically to tell me that she and Bobby had had an accident. She didn't know whether to call me or 911. She said she couldn't find him."

What Bobby's girlfriend meant by not being able to find him Peggy couldn't figure out, but she knew the dream was something other than a regular dream because, she said, "It had a big impact on me, far more than a regular dream would, and when I awakened—I was crying—I remembered the whole thing. Usually I just remember a fragment of a dream."

Peggy knew instinctively that the dream was somehow based in reality. But what could she do? Robert was in some kind of peril, and though this sense of danger hovered in her mind, she had no idea how to protect him. She didn't know what kind of an accident it was she feared, nor did she know where the danger was coming from. But on the day the accident was to occur she felt terror and dread right from the start. "I felt like I was going to jump out of my skin," she said.

All day Peggy debated whether to call Robert at his landscaping job and make special arrangements to protect him, but she didn't want to embarrass him with her maternal concern. Besides, she knew he wouldn't have listened. So it wasn't until 5:15, getting more and more concerned, that she finally called his girlfriend's house. No one was there. "I got the answering machine," she said. "And I was afraid."

Not long after—at around 6:30—Peggy got "the call." It was horrific.

As it happened, Bobby's girlfriend was on the cell phone with her brother, Jim, when the accident occurred. The cell phone was knocked out of June's hand into the back of the KIA, but it did not shut off. Jim heard the crash and alerted his mother, who continued to listen on the phone. She was actually able to hear the EMS technicians come on the scene and begin ministering to the young couple. June's mother then used another phone to call Peggy and tell her what she was overhearing, and alert her that she needed to get to the hospital immediately.

Peggy had had her "premonition" dream a couple of weeks before Robert died, and her first one after his crossing over oc-

---

Psychic dreams usually occur within close proximity of an event.

---

curred just two days after that event. She was having a horrific time with Robert's death, and had been up for countless hours. "Finally," she said, "I had fallen asleep from exhaustion. Then the dream came. In it I was sitting on a bed, and Robert was sitting right next to me. We were in my room, which was dark, but I could see his face clearly—his beautiful blue eyes, his handsome face. He rested his head on my right shoulder and I stroked his beautiful brown hair. He was crying and I started to cry too. 'Mom,' he said, 'it hurts so much to be without you.'

"I continued to stroke his hair—it was so, so soft—and my heart was breaking. I told him that we couldn't change what had happened, that we had to bear it. God, I could feel his closeness," Peggy said. The dream lasted about ten minutes, and then Robert left, telling his mother that he had to go see his Aunt Shirley. Peggy saw significance in this. "Twenty-one years earlier my Aunt Shirley had lost her son Dan in a car accident, and I thought that maybe Robert was going to be with her and him."

Peggy had two more psychic dreams after Robert's passing. In one of the dreams, which occurred about six months after he had passed, Robert was only ten or eleven years old. "I was thrilled," Peggy said. "He was wearing a blue suit and he told me, among other things, that he had come back to spend the day with me and his grandparents. And he did. It was terrific." Again, Peggy had a strong feeling it was a psychic dream and, more than that, there was the color of the sun. Says Peggy, "Rob came to me in my garden and the scene was ordinary in every way—the grass was green, the flowers colorful—except that the sun was not yellow as it should have been. It was white. Pure, brilliant white. The entire garden was bathed with a pure white light that I had never seen before, inside or outside a dream."

A few months later, in what Peggy called her "college campus" dream, she was looking out over what looked like a college campus, with broad swaths of green grass, and again she tapped into this incredible white light. "There were people walking up and down along the grass, one of whom was Robert. I was able to see his face up close, like when a camera zooms in. He looked very peaceful, just like the other people." The day was sunny, but once again the sun was not yellow. The place was beautifully illuminated as if by a bright sun, but the light was pure white. "The light was *so* bright," Peggy said. "But it didn't hurt my eyes."

That was no ordinary white light. That was Heaven, and Peggy had caught a glimpse.

YOUR PSYCHIC ABILITY

We are all psychic, but that doesn't mean we all come into our psychic ability at the same time—or that we all accept that ability. Psychic ability can emerge, like other talents, at any point in your life. For me it was when I was young, for others it may be in response to stress, or it might have a physical trigger, like an accident. The most important thing to cultivating the psychic in you is first to recognize its presence. Only then can you begin to hone it.

For starters, ask yourself some questions. Sit down in a quiet spot and think back over your life and try to remember experiences that were psychic in nature.

- Were there times in your life when you unaccountably *just knew* something?
- Have there been instances when you modified your behavior for no logical reason—with important results?
- Was there a time when you believed that you had a psychic dream?
- Did you ever dismiss a color or light that perhaps might have been an aura?
- Have you seen the dead or signs of them? Did they speak to you?
- Have you ever dreamed about an event that had nothing to do with you—and then learned it came true?
- Have you ever thought that you had a sixth sense about people?
- Have you ever made a successful business decision based on a hunch?
- Have you ever known the phone or doorbell was going to ring—and then it did?

Recalling such things will not be easy and, indeed, you might find yourself looking for a psychic needle in a haystack. Our brains are filled with millions of experiences. Sorting through them to discern what's psychic and what's not is going to take effort. You'll have to think about it, so try not to get discouraged when you don't come up with something right away. Be willing to think about it again—and again.

Some people, of course, will not want to do it. Not because

they dislike hard work (though some do), but because they'll have rejected the whole notion of being psychic. These are the same people—and I don't mean to criticize, just tell the truth—who could never imagine that the world was round, or that men could fly, or that a living creature could be created by cloning.

Years ago I was subjected to a blistering attack by a skeptical radio talk show host named Candy Jones, who questioned whether everyone has psychic ability. My answer—still my answer to skeptics—is a question: How can you say it doesn't exist unless you try to experience it yourself? If you are not willing to try, then you have no factual basis for your conclusion. To put this another way, don't decide it before you try it.

"How come you don't know the lottery numbers?"

One question I frequently get is if I'm so psychic why don't I guess the lottery numbers. My answer is that emotion gets in the way. I would love to win the lottery, but I could never approach it calmly and coolly, which is required for good psychic work.

Emotion colors and modifies our feelings and thoughts, and it interferes with psychic energy. If we could all just have psychic insight, which is cool and quick and very objective, we'd all be rich. Plus—and this is important—being psychic entails accountability. When you enhance your psychic powers you automatically take on some special responsibility because, for one thing, you will be seeing intensely private things about people, things that must stay private. Ethics demands it. When someone comes into my office, for example, everything they say—and I say—stays in that room unless they give me permission to reveal it.

DÉJÀ VU

- We're all born psychic, and our psychic abilities can show up at any time in our lives.
- Being psychic is all about receiving information without the use of regular thought processes. This information is contained in soul energy that comes to us through conscious and unconscious perceptions.
- Conscious psychic perceptions are thoughts that pop into our heads. We just *know* things. We may describe these perceptions in various ways, such as "a feeling," "a gut instinct," or "it's just something I sensed." But if you examine the perceptions you'll see that they're cool and quick and have little if anything to do with emotion, which is hot and often relates to desire perception.
- Unconscious perceptions are psychic thoughts we are not aware of. They enter our minds surreptitiously, and influence our decisions in significant ways. Besides not being aware of them, we have no choice between action and inaction. We are, in a way, forced to do whatever the unconscious perceptions require us to do.
- Auras are halos or clusters of light that reveal a person's essence, including health and character. They change according to emotional or physical states, and the changes can occur quickly or over a long period of time.
- The dead speak to us telepathically, which means that a thought or cluster of energy in their spirit can be transferred to us. Our sixth sense—the psychic mechanism in our brains—picks the signals up like a radio receiver and translates these messages so that we can understand them.

- Psychic information is often imparted to us in dreams, when our defenses are down. Psychic dreams normally occur soon after someone crosses over, but they can occur before as a premonition. Psychic dreams are vivid or contain unusual colors, and they may also have a special impact on the dreamer.
- To start to get a handle on your psychic side, review your own life for psychic experiences. Recognizing that you have a psychic side is key to developing it and using it.

TWO

What's In It for You?

AVOIDING DANGER

Virginia Haber was summoned into her boss's office.

"I've got a problem, Ginny," he said. "Dave Andrews was supposed to go to Atlanta at the end of the week to finalize the Morkar deal, but he's in the hospital with appendicitis. I need you to go there for him."

"No problem," she said. And for her it wasn't. Virginia is a take-charge type of person. An executive for a midlevel import-export firm in Miami, she was used to working under pressure. Virginia went back to her own office and told her secretary to get her a flight to Atlanta in time for a Sunday morning breakfast meeting with Morkar. That done, she went to Dave Andrews's office and instructed his secretary to start putting together the necessary documents for her meeting.

When she left the office at around 9 P.M., Virginia had the Morkar contracts in her attaché case, her flight to Atlanta was set, and she was looking forward to the drive home. Twelve-hour days and six- and sometimes seven-day weeks were usual for Virginia, and she had learned to use the half-hour drive to her home in Hollywood productively, listening to classical music and winding down from her workday.

Virginia got into her car, which was in the company parking lot, settled in behind the wheel, started it up, and cranked up the air-conditioning. Then, just as she was about to turn on the radio, a barely detectable idea floated across her mind. She pulled her hand away from the radio, sat back, and tried to determine exactly what the idea was. She realized it was an intuitive idea, one that comes out of nowhere, but she couldn't figure out more than that. At first it was a wisp of nothing, a sort of whisper. But very quickly she understood. It was a warning. It said that she should not take the flight to Atlanta, that it was perilous. Virginia understood intuition. She had used it in business as well as in her personal life; nevertheless, she immediately dismissed this warning as illogical. Virginia had been flying since she was in college out in the Midwest. She had so many frequent-flier miles piled up that it would be years before she would have to pay for a vacation. Her husband Ray had once commented, "The only people who fly more than you, Ginny, are the pilots." Occasionally, she knew, planes crashed, but she also knew that statistically flying was the safest mode of travel. Moreover, she simply was not afraid. Flying was to Virginia what car travel was to most people, an everyday experience which she hardly ever thought about. In fact, she now stopped thinking about it. She turned on the soothing music and started home.

At home that night, after a pleasant supper with Ray, Virginia went into her office to go over papers relevant to the Morkar trip.

Suddenly there was another thought, another out-of-the-blue intuitive idea that told her not to go to Atlanta. This time a little trickle of fear was attached. Virginia analyzed her fear. Maybe, she thought, it was related to a rather scary newspaper story she had read a while back about airplane hijackers. Maybe she was unconsciously afraid of them. Or maybe it was related to something else. Maybe she really resented having to do someone else's work, spending time in Atlanta that could be much better spent at her office, or with Ray. Or, maybe she was unconsciously afraid to face the situation she was flying into. It didn't take Virginia long to decide that that last Freudian insight didn't hold any water. The meeting was with a client who had a twenty-five-year relationship with her company and the business itself was to be really quite routine, just dotting all the "i's" and crossing all the "t's" of a very ordinary contract.

Unable to talk herself out of her anxiety, Virginia went to bed with the fear. The next morning when she awoke and the concern was still there—albeit diminished—Virginia decided on another tack. She always started her day with exercise, so she would just increase it. Hopefully, she could sweat off the anxiety. She doubled her sit-ups, did some extra squatting exercises, and quite a dramatic change, walked four miles through the streets of Hollywood, instead of her usual two. No mean feat considering the humidity in the city. When Virginia completed her 6 A.M. walk she was soaked to the skin. But the exercise was good and she was pleased when the fear subsided.

Unfortunately, the anxiety did return at random moments during the day. Each time the fear came back, Virginia tried to attach the feeling to an idea she could try to deal with. Maybe the flight date, May 11, had some hidden, fearful significance to her. Maybe it was the type of plane, a DC9, she was scheduled to fly on. She used her quite powerful intelligence to try to open the door to the source of her fears, but was unsuccessful. She briefly considered asking her doctor to prescribe a tranquilizer, but discarded that notion. Virginia regarded her body as something of a temple. What was more, she was a fighter. She didn't want her fear to beat her.

Nothing in life is to be feared.
It is only to be understood.
—Marie Curie

The next day the warnings became more strident. "Don't go," said the little voice. "Don't go." Virginia's fear ratcheted upward. She started to think about rescheduling—she knew that Morkar would likely go along with whatever she wanted—when that thought was interrupted by a new idea that enlarged her fear even more. This thought said that she wouldn't arrive at Atlanta International Airport. Virginia interpreted *wouldn't arrive* to mean a plane crash. And she was terrified.

All these ideas combined into a sort of juggernaut in her mind, a force that said: *Don't take the flight you're scheduled on to Atlanta.*

"I couldn't dismiss the voice anymore," Virginia said. "So I acted instead. I called Morkar and told him that the eleventh would be a little difficult for me. Would he mind if I rescheduled?"

Of course he didn't, so I then changed the flight to arrive on the evening of the tenth, one day before I was originally scheduled to leave. The moment I made the change, the fear disappeared.

"It was miraculous," Virginia said. "It just vanished in an instant."

Very often we act on our psychic side and don't really find out the reason behind our actions or the "what if" that would have taken place had we not changed our plans. But Virginia did. She was scheduled to take ValuJet flight 592, which lifted off from Miami International Airport on May 11, 1996, with 110 passengers aboard. Eighteen minutes later the plane crashed in the Florida Everglades and all 110 souls crossed over. If she had not changed the date, Virginia's next stop would have been eternity.

Virginia's psychic side had saved her life

When she had first heard *the little voice,* she disregarded its validity. But when it persisted, Virginia decided to pay attention. "I guess I came to realize that I shouldn't ignore an intuition that I almost always listened to in business and other affairs. Why would the voice be *less* important because it was telling me how to save my life? It was the same voice—it just had something different to say than usual."

Many people use their psychic ability, particularly their intuition, to avoid danger. Cops and moms in particular. As one cop said to me, "When you approach a dark house in the middle of the night and there's been a report of an intruder, all kinds of thoughts run through your mind. Sure, your training kicks in as to the proper approach. But the greatest friend cops have in dangerous situations is intuition. We've all learned how to listen to that feel-

---

So, *what's in it for you?* A lot. At its most dramatic, your innate psychic ability can help keep you out of harm's way. There are other benefits too, more common, such as navigating the romantic seas, making more astute career moves, bettering your business abilities, solving apparently insolvable problems, and getting in touch with your spiritual side.

---

ing that just sort of comes up. I can tell you this: Because of intuition a lot of cops who otherwise would not be are walking around."

Everyone knows that moms are veritable seismographs who can sense any deviation on the Richter scale of their kids' behavior. But I'm not talking about that here. I'm talking about the ideas that pop up without any logical preamble. For example, a woman I know told me that one day she was in the kitchen washing dishes when she sensed that her two-year-old daughter, Mary, was in grave danger. Mary was supposed to be in her bedroom down the hall. Her mother didn't hear any sounds of her coming from the room, but it wasn't the silence that bothered her. As she explained: "Mary was always a quiet child, but this was different—something told me that she was in danger. I wondered how. There was nothing dangerous in the room. It contained her crib, her child-proofed toys, a rug on the floor, the outlets covered with safety plates.

"But that little voice in me would not go away. I dried my hands and went down the hall. When I entered Mary's room the sight almost made me freeze. Mary was standing by an open window—this was four flights up—opening a box of Band-Aids. I smiled through my terror, managed a 'Hi, honey' and approached her very slowly and gently until I could gently guide her away from the window and close it.

"Later, I asked my two older kids how the window had gotten open and no one seemed to know, but I had my suspicions. Still, if my intuition had not told me to go into that room, who knew if Mary's next step would have been to climb up on the windowsill to get a good look out the window? The scene still gives me a hollow feeling in my stomach."

I've used intuition myself many times, but one event in particular stands out in my mind. I was twelve. My mother and I had just moved to Astoria, Queens, which was a far cry from where we used to live in Islip. Astoria really is part of "The City," which is a nickname for New York City, and as such, had its share of drugs, crimes, and violence. Anyway, the event occurred on a very hot,

---

The intellect has little to do on the road to discovery. There comes a leap in consciousness, call it intuition or what you will, and the solution comes to you and you don't know how or why.

—Albert Einstein

---

muggy day in July. Standard summer in the city weather. I was strolling down a broad avenue named Ditmars Boulevard near where I lived. There was nothing to be afraid of on Ditmars. The street was very ordinary, flanked with stores—bakeries, gas stations, cleaners, etc.—and dotted with very ordinary pedestrians. Everything was fine until I got to around Twenty-sixth Street, when a thought occurred to me: I was in danger.

This notion came to me in a cool, calm "just-the-facts-ma'am" style. It told me to turn around and go back the other way, not to go any closer to Twenty-ninth Street. I had heard this little psychic voice for years and I knew it didn't lie. Still, illogically, my logical mind started to pepper my psychic side with questions, which all boiled down to one question: How are you in danger?

I speculated. Was a car going to veer off the road and run over me? Was somebody going to drop a piano off the roof on me? Was there going to be an explosion in one of the stores where I would be caught in the blast? Was a bolt of lightning going to incinerate me? I smiled at the last speculation. The lightning, I thought, would have to come from a special place because the sky was now pure powder blue, the only clouds in it a few wisps of white.

Still, despite the semi-sarcastic questioning of my logical mind, my psychic side won. I did an about face and walked quickly away. Thank God. The next day I heard on the radio that there had been a ferocious gang fight on Twenty-ninth Street and my timing would have been perfect—or imperfect. I would have walked right into the thick of it. Four people were in the hospital and one person, a kid close to my age, was in the morgue.

The thing about acting on your psychic intuition is that you don't always find out about the danger you may have escaped. But trust your instinct and you won't go wrong. There's no question about it: Disregard the advice of your psychic side at your own peril. That little voice is borne of psychic energy from someone who loves you. Be aware of it. And trust.

ROMANTIC RELATIONSHIPS

Like so many people, I got into my life's work by accident. Or so it would seem. Actually, I believe that the path I took in life, like others, was predetermined. Every soul has a blueprint, and this is mine.

For me, it all began in the early eighties when I matriculated at St. John's University. I enrolled in a pre-law course and had also snared an after-school job in a big Manhattan law office. At first glance, it looked like I was sitting pretty, definitely on my way to achieving my goal in life, which was to get a law degree and then go overseas to use my legal prowess and know-how to help people who were less fortunate than I. But the time I spent in the law office was eye-opening—and dispiriting. I witnessed so many instances of people lacking integrity, morality, and ethics that after a year I knew that being an attorney was not for me. Sadly, I turned away and switched to hospital administration. I figured that when I graduated I could hook up with a hospital and find ample opportunity to satisfy my yearning to help people. It was at the school of hospital administration that I met Victoria Soho, who was to be the catalyst for my career.

Victoria was sweet and smart and oh-so-beautiful. Her heritage was a startling mix of French and Hispanic. She had dark, liquid eyes; wavy, luxuriant raven hair; a perfect complexion; and a lovely figure. She was the kind of woman that gives men a

"7-Eleven" (Big Gulp) reaction: when they see her they fall in love. But for some reason—I have no idea why—I didn't fall in love with Victoria. Instead I formed a deep friendship with her which was built on long and sometimes painful talks.

For one thing, Victoria was trying to cope with the death of her mother, Rita. To help her, I was forced to reveal my psychic side, the side that could bring the dead into the room and have a conversation. When I detailed to Victoria what I could do, she was very accepting and believing. And she was not surprised when I was able to connect with Rita and carry some wonderful news to Victoria. Her mother was doing fine and wanted to tell Victoria to stop worrying about her. And she did.

But Victoria had a darker problem. Her boyfriend, Jim, was abusive. After hearing a catalog of his abuse, which included hitting and choking her, I put the problem to her mother. Her advice was pointed: "Get rid of the bum!"

I relayed this to Victoria, and encouraged her to split from Jim. She avoided doing it two or three times, but one night she gritted her teeth and told him flat out that they were finished. Jim acted predictably: He became enraged. For a time Victoria told me she didn't know if she would be able to stand up to him and would have to "take him back." But I—and her mom—greatly encouraged her to stand by her guns. And one day Jim went away and didn't come back.

My relationship with Victoria went deeper than just telling her that I was a closet psychic. I also told her how I didn't know where I fit in the world or, and this was very painful, if I did fit in at all. But just as I encouraged her, she encouraged me. "Just be who you are," she would say. "You have something special to offer the world, so offer it. The world is waiting for you, Jeffrey."

I used to meet Victoria in the St. Vincent's Cafeteria, one of two cafeterias that served the school population. We would have lunch together, or maybe coffee, and sometimes we'd just sit and talk. But one day when we met I sensed something different about her. And then she said:

"Can I ask you something?"

"The answer is no, Vicki. We're not meant to be married!"

She laughed.

"No," she said. "I'm very proud of you and your abilities. Do you mind if I tell some of my sisters about you?" Vicki was a member of a sorority and many of her sorority sisters hung around the cafeteria.

Logically, I should have answered "No" because, of course, all my life I had hidden my abilities. But I sensed that that time was past, and that it was time to try out what my first psychic mentor Joanie Lopez, had said to me when I was seven years old: "Some day you'll be like me, Jeffrey. It's your calling. But you'll also be famous."

It was useless to fight. I am what I am.

"Yes," I said simply, "you can."

Vicki didn't have to tell me she did it. I would be sitting at the cafeteria table and catch a girl glancing at me, or maybe staring, or scoping me out with her peripheral vision. I was well aware that I was getting attention I had never gotten before.

Then, the inevitable happened. One day I was in the cafeteria having my usual cup of coffee and reading one of my textbooks when a thin, pale-faced girl with long blonde tangled hair and light, troubled eyes sat down opposite me and nervously smiled. She wasn't unfamiliar to me. Twice before I had noticed that she had been watching me closely, and I knew, psychically, that this meeting was destined.

"You're Jeffrey, right?"

"That's me."

"I'm Janet Gilchrist," she said. "I heard about you from Victoria. I understand that you're a psychic."

"I play around with it."

"Could you help me?"

"You mean," I said, "help with your problems with your boyfriend, Ernie." The rest of the blood drained out of her already pale face.

"Yes. I'm willing to pay. How much would you charge?"

I had no idea. But I plucked a figure out of midair that seemed fair.

"Twenty dollars."

"Okay."

I nodded.

"And your fundamental problem with him is that he is usually living in his own world—without you."

"That's right," she said, "that's so right." And then frustration and anger and hurt boiled up and gushed out of her, and she rapidly detailed how Ernie would choose to be with his friends rather than her. If they wanted to go to a ballgame, and she wanted to go to a movie, he'd choose the ballgame. If they were going to play cards and she wanted to just take a ride with him, the card game won. If she wanted to have dinner and his friends wanted to go to the bar, he'd go to the bar. "I'm not second fiddle with him," she said, "I'm third fiddle."

While she was talking, a dead person appeared behind her, a small woman wearing a green sweater and black pants with short gray hair and a face with a certain set to her jaw that said the tougher it got the more she liked it. I described her to Janet. "That sounds like my Aunt Alice," Janet said.

"Well," I said, "Aunt Alice is incensed with the way Ernie is treating you, and she has this advice: Next time Ernie makes you play third fiddle, tell him you don't want to see him anymore unless you will come first. Period."

"I don't think I can do that," Janet said.

"Aunt Alice says you can."

A few weeks later Janet sat down opposite me in the St. Vincent's Cafeteria. Right away I noticed important differences in her physical appearance. Her hair was brushed and neat. The dark circles under her eyes had paled somewhat, and she seemed to have more color in her face. She looked like she had put on a couple of pounds and joy came off her like heat.

"It worked," she said, smiling. "Real well!"

"How so?"

"Well, for one thing now he calls me first to find out what I'm doing, and he wants to be with me more or less all the time. I've seen him five nights this past week, and he's called me a dozen times. He told me flat out that I am the 'Number one priority' in his life and he will never 'dis' me again. He told me that I scared him, that he's crazy about me, and that I taught him a lesson he won't forget."

"I wish Aunt Alice would appear," I said. "But I'll bet you she's smiling!"

It wasn't long before my success with Janet had been tele-

How many times have you had an intuition about someone—then ignored it?

---

typed around the school and more and more sorority sisters, and then non-sorority sisters, started to sit down opposite me. At twenty dollars a pop I was doing very well for a formerly impoverished college student, thank you very much! After a while I became so busy that I had to expand the readings to after-school hours. For these I used my basement apartment, which was part of a single-family home which I shared with a fellow student named Neil. The apartment had two advantages. It was within walking distance of St. John's, and it was cheap. But there the advantages ceased. The apartment contained only two rooms, one for Neil and one for me, a kitchen, and an oversize walk-in closet which the enterprising and chutzpah-laden landlord had, almost unbelievably, rented out as living quarters to some student athletes before us. The bathroom, reminiscent of some turn-of-the-century tenement, was outside in a hall. And as if that wasn't bad enough, there was a constant buzz from a leather processing sweatshop which the landlord had built next to the basement. The only viable place where I could do my readings was in the kitchen. To insure privacy, I only conducted them when Neil wasn't around.

Back then, 85 percent of my clients were female. Today that has changed to a rough 50/50 split. But what has not changed are the concerns of clients, and leading the parade is romantic relationships. People want to know the same things today as they did yesterday: Am I really in love? Should I be in love? Does my partner love me? Is my partner being unfaithful?

I have given many people advice in this area, and you can use your own psychic ability to administer advice to yourself. Just remember to listen to the little voice, or whatever psychic input you get. If you receive a psychic message that tells you you'll never be happy with a particular person, believe it. Look for the signs. Listen for the voice. Trust it. And act on it. You may just surprise yourself.

MAKING BETTER CAREER MOVES

Hone your psychic ability and you can learn to make the career moves that are right for you. And you may be in for a revelation. When I was at college I gave my fellow students all kinds of advice about what curricula to pursue to further their careers, some of which seemed quite bizarre at the time. I remember telling one student named Joe (a tough guy from Brooklyn whose speech was loaded with "dees" and "dems") something that shocked him immensely:

"I'm being told by your uncle Vito," I said, "that you would make a great horse trainer."

"Are you kidding?"

"No. That's what he's telling me."

Joe was about to object again but paused.

"You know," he said, "my great-grandfather used to train horses in Italy."

"There you go."

"It does sound crazy though. I'm training to be a phys ed teacher."

"I know, but you're not totally against the idea are you?"

"No?"

The psychic seed had been planted. Joe thought about it, and realized that such a course of action might just be the right one for him. Eventually, he became a full-time horse trainer in Old Westbury, New York.

I bring this anecdote to emphasize a point: When you use your psychic side to access career information you may well get answers that don't seem to coincide with your training and background. Don't be shocked if job suggestions seem bizarre. Take them as they come. Listen to the psychic clues and use your best judgment. And take your time. After you've learned how to develop your psychic side, you'll be better able to distinguish between psychic information and just plain fancy. So if you get an inkling that you should be a pearl diver in Fiji, consider the source before you pack your bags!

Your soul mission is your reason for being, your life purpose. It's your calling in life—who you feel called to be, what you feel called to do.

—Alan Seale

BETTER BUSINESS SENSE

Psychic ability can be a great ally in business situations. Better information leads to sounder decisions. And in some cases—though not everyone can do it—you may even be able to visualize people who you've never seen and get a psychological "read" on them before you meet.

About seven years ago, for example, I represented a small manufacturer of auto parts who was negotiating a deal with a larger manufacturer. Before the principals arrived, I tried to visualize people from the larger company and I was able to see and sense the president, who was almost exactly like the person who came into the room to meet my client. Unfortunately, my premonition was correct and this man was *not* a quality person.

"Hi," he said, "I'm Dirk Andrews. How are you fine folks today?"

Dirk looked like a security operative in Las Vegas. He had on a sharkskin suit, a high quality toupee, caps on his teeth, a store-bought tan, and rings on all but two of his fingers. I shook his hand and said to myself: "Oh yeah, Dirk, I know you. We've met already."

The exterior package, in this case, defined the man. Dirk was as phony as a three-dollar bill. His purpose, I intuited, was to gather important financial data on the company in preparation for a hostile and not so scrupulous takeover. And I was right. Eight months later, Dirk was indicted on several counts of fraud.

Being able to visualize and get a sense of what someone is like might seem like a Herculean feat. But as you develop your psychic skills, it's just one more great thing you'll be able to do. Make no mistake about it, though. Psychic energy, the fundamental stuff that allows us to transmit information, is powerful in the same way an electrical current is powerful. More powerful, in fact. You can't see it but if you get in its way you'll surely know it. I just don't want you to be surprised one day if things start breaking, shaking, and moving while you're in psychic action.

About ten years ago I was called in to consult on a business deal by a friend of mine named Laurie, who was involved in making sports movies. Laurie was hooked up with a world renowned female Olympic long-distance runner and a guy I'll call Ted, who had played minor league baseball and who, purportedly, was loaded with investment cash.

My role was twofold. I have a pretty good head for business, so Laurie asked me if I would give her my take on how things stacked up financially. But she mainly wanted me there because I was a psychic. Hopefully I would be able to read Ted and see if he was for real or not, and whether the deal was worth embarking on.

Laurie, Ted, and I met at the upscale George Washington Manor in Roslyn, New York. We filed into the posh room and took seats around a large satiny conference table on which—and this is relevant—was a thick, dark green candle about 8 inches high between me and the young investor. I was introduced to everyone as Laurie's accountant, which would allow me to logically ask probing, intrusive questions. And hard questions were in order. A lot of money was involved, as well as the reputation of a world-class Olympic runner. We had to uncover the truth, whatever it was.

We sat around the table for a few minutes engaged in small talk and surface camaraderie, a common thing people do before a meeting to bleed off nervousness. I was not nervous, but I was intense—intensely focused on Ted. I knew I had to watch myself because I didn't want to scare him into lockjaw. I consciously tried to relax my facial muscles, look this way and that and, perhaps most important, not stare at Ted. Many people have told me, and I know it to be true, that my hazel eyes are "piercing."

Small talk behind us, the meeting really began and I started questioning Ted. I noticed, as he answered the questions, that his light blue eyes were on the intense side too. And why not? He was being grilled.

Ted was being straightforward, answering my questions in a decisive and favorable manner. I was being very direct, and very incisive, as was Ted, who was matching my gaze with one of his own. Well, everything was proceeding as it should when suddenly, without warning, the thick green candle ripped down the middle, the two halves falling away as if split by an invisible ax. Everyone was stunned. "What had caused the candle to divide?" they all asked, bewildered.

I knew what had happened. My psychic energy, with perhaps Ted's energy bolstering it, had severed the candle.

The meeting continued for another fifteen minutes and then ended, but well before that I knew no deal was going to happen. And it had nothing to do with Ted—who I got good answers and good vibes from—or the Olympic runner. It was because my friend Laurie, the meeting revealed, did not have the necessary know-how or production savvy to make it all work. She would be going into something that was way over her head. Ted and Laurie promised to "get back" to one another, but I knew they wouldn't.

We all went down on the elevator together, and as we walked across the parking lot in the cool night to our respective cars I started to walk next to Ted.

"I wanted to tell you something," I said.

"What's that?"

"I'm a psychic. I was hired to evaluate you."

Ted laughed. "Why are you telling me now?"

"I have no idea," I said. "I guess it's because I like you and want to be upfront." We both laughed hard. I wanted to tell him, in a roundabout way, that he would make a fine partner. What I didn't tell him was that I (and possibly he) was responsible for the cloven candle.

True to what I sensed, the deal never came to pass. Years later, however, I came across Ted's name in the financial section of *The New York Times*. He had become a very successful investment banker and would have, indeed, made a good partner.

JUST FOR FUN

When I was young I was terrified of being ridiculed, so I hid my paranormal abilities. That didn't mean I didn't use them. Or that I didn't have fun!

I was a very active sandlot player as a kid, and I would predict to myself who would win our games, who would screw up, and who would be the hero. Rarely would I make a prediction for all to hear or let my friends spot a premonition on my face. I didn't want anyone to pick up a pattern of paranormal activity.

I remember one baseball game we had for the "All Astoria" neighborhood championship. I sure wished I had told one guy of my premonition—maybe it wouldn't have come true. At the start of the game I visualized our usually flawless shortstop, Artie, muffing a simple grounder in the ninth inning.

When we reached the bottom of the ninth we were ahead by just one run, with the other team batting. They had a guy on second and one on third, with two out. The batter swung at the first pitch and, what do you know, smacked a hard but routine grounder toward Artie.

Sure enough, the ball went right through Artie's legs and both runners scored. "There goes the championship," we all groaned.

I don't know if it qualifies as fun—some people may say it's more like grand theft—but it made me feel good when I was able to use my psychic sensibility on my schoolwork at college. Once I was having a good deal of trouble with a test I was taking in government and politics. I was struggling with the works of Plato, one of the most complicated philosophers, when all of a sudden, a dead person appeared. I had no idea who he was, but he had bulbous eyes, a pencil thin moustache above a generous mouth, and

---

Every person, all the events of your life, are there because you have drawn them there. What you choose to do with them is up to you.

—Richard Bach

---

long dark hair. He was dressed in the kind of fine clothes they wore in Europe in the seventeenth and eighteenth centuries. Immediately he started to give me the answers I needed—in French. Now, I don't ordinarily speak French, but somehow I was able to understand, and I wrote his answers to the questions in English. Verbatim. When I had answered all the questions—or rather, when *he* had answered all the questions—and was leaving the room, a name came to mind: René Descartes, the seventeenth-century philosopher and one of the greatest who ever lived.

The next week, though, I got an unpleasant surprise. My professor had marked Descartes's answers as wrong. I didn't know what to do. I couldn't very well go up to him and say: "But René Descartes answered these." But what I did do was tell the teacher that I thought that I saw the interpretations I had in a book by Descartes. The professor said he would check into it, and the next week he told me he agreed that I was right. Or, rather, I thought, Descartes was. Anyway, the teacher changed my mark. "*Merci*, René," I thought, "*merci!*"

SOLVING INSOLUBLE ISSUES

All this fun and gathering info is great, but some people would say that the most important psychic benefit comes from solving issues that seem insoluble. Consider the plight of Jackie Bergin, a middle-aged postal employee from Spotswood, New Jersey. One day in September of 2001 Jackie was informed by police that her only son, Michael, thirty-three, had killed himself. Following instructions given in a manual provided by the Hemlock Society, he had gone into a closet with a hibachi filled with charcoal, closed the door, and lit the charcoal, which gave off carbon monoxide and killed him. Investigation revealed that Michael was in despair because he had lost, in short order, his long-time girlfriend and his job.

"After the funeral service, I climbed into bed and just couldn't get out," Jackie was to tell me. "I couldn't go to work, I couldn't eat, I just wanted to die, go home to Michael, and hold him in my arms."

Her family convinced her to see a psychiatrist, and she did, but it didn't help. The psychiatrist, as good as he was, couldn't bring back Michael. Jackie quit, and then went back to bed. And then one day in December of 2001, her sister, who was watching TV in Jackie's house, came into the bedroom.

"Hey Jackie," she said, "get up and watch this guy. He's helping people just like you on *The Maury Show.*"

The guy was me, and Jackie did get up to watch. Her sister suggested she see me professionally, and she agreed. But that's easier said than done. I'm ordinarily booked with clients over a year in advance. But on this one day, twenty minutes before she called I had a cancellation, which is very rare for me. Happily, I penciled in Jackie's name, and she got in her car and traveled the two and a half hours from New Jersey to see me in my Port Washington office.

Some twenty minutes into our consultation Michael came into the office and stood behind his mother. "He has something to tell you," I said.

"I'm very sorry for what I did," Michael, obviously distraught, told me. "The last thing I wanted to do was make you suffer. Please don't suffer, Mom. I'm okay. I'm okay. I'm with Grandma and Grandpa and I want you to look for me every day, because I'm going to give you signs that I'm with you. And please don't worry about the way I died. I'm okay now—really."

When Michael was finished, tears were streaming down Jackie's face, but she was smiling.

"Do you know that this is the first time I've smiled in over a year?" she said.

I smiled myself.

"You saved my life."

"No, I didn't," I said, "Michael did that. He loves you very, very much."

From time to time I hear from Jackie, who is now retired, and is also an advocate for suicide prevention. And, yes, from time to time she sees signs of Michael. He's around her, and she knows it.

SPIRITUAL DEVELOPMENT

Using our psychic side can help us to develop spiritually. Once we are able to listen to voices and interpret signs of the dead, we can realize that the dead are souls that never die. Moreover, we can understand that we are just the same, souls in transit to the other side. Those of us who have passed are on their way to the light, the particular Heavenworld they believe in. Some day we will be there too.

These realizations are profound and can put everything in life in perspective. They can give us a higher purpose, a concern both outside and greater than ourselves. In essence—and I don't hold myself up as a theologian—we become more like the God that we worship. What could be more important?

DÉJÀ VU

- Tapping into your psychic ability may help you to avoid danger, improve your romantic relationships, make better career and business decisions, resolve problems, and give you a greater understanding of your place in the universe.
- Often when you act on your psychic side you won't know the danger you escaped or the benefit you have invited. That's even more reason to value your psychic ability. Listen and trust. You can't go wrong.
- Psychic energy can be as powerful as an electric current. Respect this power. Don't abuse it.
- Understanding and interpreting psychic communications can help you to realize that the dead are souls that never die. Your psychic side really can help you to appreciate the scope and beauty of the universe.

THREE

Understanding the Dead

MESSAGES FROM THE DEAD

I had my first visit from a dead person when I was seven and still living with my mom in a garden apartment in Islip. I remember the visit clearly, which is not surprising since I had the bejeebbers scared out of me.

It was dusk, a cool Friday in late October, and I was doing something that was unusual for me: watching television. Usually I liked to read baseball adventure books. Looking back, I'm sure that I had received an unconscious psychic message to be in the room at this time, that I was going to get a visitor.

Anyway, I was lying belly down on my bed, facing the TV, a small black-and-white job that was on a dresser with a mirror attached. To the left of the dresser an open door led to a hallway and other rooms in the house—kitchen, bathroom, dining, and living rooms. I could hear the click and clack of my mother working in the kitchen and could smell the tangy aroma of the tacos she was making. I felt very safe. And very hungry.

Suddenly, a chill. I turned around, sensing that someone had entered the room and was standing behind me. No one was there. Still, I felt scared. When I looked back I saw something in my right peripheral vision. My eyes flicked to the corner and I nearly wet myself. There she was. An old lady. And she was looking right at me.

I had no idea who this old lady was. She was dressed in a long-sleeved blue dress and brown stockings that were rolled up at the knees. Her gray hair was in a bun and she had a prominent chin and very intense eyes. I wanted to call my mother to help me but I was frozen. All I could do was stare.

Then, the old lady spoke to me. But not in a normal sense. There was no sound. No language. She had a thought which was transferred to my head via her energy—later I identified this as telepathy—and I understood her.

"Don't be afraid," she said. "I won't harm you. My name is Mary and I once had children just like you. George and Michael and Trevor and others. I had twelve children."

Nothing threatening. Still, I couldn't respond.

"I am your spirit guide, and I will help you all the days of your life."

Then, without saying another word, she walked from the corner, past the dresser, then turned at the doorway and started to go down the hall. I wanted to yell to my mother to watch out but couldn't. Part way down the hall, before she was fully out of my line of sight, the old lady disappeared. Ten seconds later my mother was standing in the doorway. She didn't seem upset or disturbed in any way.

"Time to eat, Jeffrey."

I finally found my voice.

"Did you see the lady?"

"What lady?"

"A lady came into the room and spoke to me. She told me she was my guide."

As I spoke, my mother's expression settled into a look of disbelief. Clearly she thought I was a little kid in fantasyland.

A few days later, my maternal grandparents called us from their home in Hamilton, Ontario, something they did twice a week. I loved it when they called. A couple of years earlier I had spent many months with them when my mother was going through some unspecified "trouble," and I enjoyed it very much. When my mother was finished talking I got on the phone with my grandmother. I felt an urge to explain what had happened. When I was finished she was quiet for a moment and then said:

"You know who that was?"

"No."

"That was your great grandmother. Mary—my mother."

"Oh," I said, neither surprised nor shocked. I was too young to understand what she had said, just what the implication of "great grandmother" was. Years later, I was to learn that when my great grandmother Mary appeared to me she had been dead twenty-three years.

My great grandmother had appeared to me in full human form. But after Mary's first appearance I started to receive visits from other dead people and they appeared in other forms as well. In the daytime, for example, they would often appear as orbs or flashes of light; just a quick something out of the side of my eye. At night, they would show up as shadows moving quickly across the room or inside my closet. They scared the hell out of me, and I usually dealt with their appearances by pulling the covers up over my head and hoping they'd go away.

The "Light People," as I called my visitors, often let me know

---

What is significant in psychic life always lies below the horizon of consciousness.

—Carl Jung

---

they were around by making noise, or by touching me, which was particularly unsettling. My first experience of this kind occurred in the middle of the night. I was in my room. The light was on as usual. I awakened, aware that something was poking me in the leg. At first I thought I was having a dream. But if it was a dream, I thought, wouldn't there be images? But there were no images. Just the poking. I tried to keep my eyes shut, but the poking got stronger, more insistent. I sat up straight, and I realized it had stopped.

I got out of bed and walked around the room. The closet door was closed but I opened it and looked in. Nothing. I looked under the bed. Also nothing. Maybe, I thought, my mother had done it. It had taken me a while to wake up, so maybe I didn't see her. I had no idea why she would be poking me, still . . . I hoped. I went out of my bedroom and stood in the open doorway to her room, which was adjacent to mine. The light was off but I could make out my mom's form under the covers. It hadn't been her. I went back into my room, back to bed, and fell asleep. Again, I felt the poking. This time it was really strong. But when I looked no one was there, and I got it: It was the Light People. Then, they disappeared.

The dead don't always have important messages to share. Sometimes they just want to have fun!

One time these Light People pulled something that was very annoying. It occurred one very cold February night when my room, despite the heat being turned on high, was chilly. I was nestled under the blankets. Even my head was covered. Suddenly, I felt the covers being pulled off me. I poked my head, turtlelike, out from under the covers and expected to see my mother playing a trick, but I saw no one.

The pulling stopped when I poked out my head, but as soon as I put my head back under the covers it started again, only this time with much more insistence. When I looked again the pulling stopped and I tried to go back to sleep. I was almost there when the covers were pulled all the way off me with a quick, ferocious yank, which scared the daylights out of me—and also pissed me off. I pulled the covers back on, and was able to get to sleep. I wasn't bothered the rest of the night. I guess the dead didn't want to mess with seven-year-old Jeffrey when he was annoyed!

The second person to appear—and also speak to me—was a friend of mine named Timmy. Timmy was a neighborhood kid, a couple of years older than I. I liked him very much. He was pudgy and funny, and we shared a love of fishing which we did at a huge lake a few hundred yards from where I lived. Timmy taught me a lot about fishing, including the fact that fishing at night was better than in the day. But night fishing was out for me. My mother would not allow it. I was just too young, she always said.

On this night, the bulb in the single lamp in my room had burned out and the room was totally dark. I awakened from a deep sleep and was stunned to see Timmy. It would have scared me enough if he was in human form, but that wasn't quite the case. He was in the outline of a human being, the lines composed of thin, delicate neon tubes, all white. There was no question it was Timmy, though. His chubby body was clearly identifiable as was his butch haircut, and the eyes, though just dots of light, were unmistakably his. I started to cry, but he told me, like my grandmother had, not to be afraid and I stopped crying.

"I just wanted to tell you, Jeffrey, that I was run over on the way to the fishing hole, but I'm okay and I'm going to the light."

I understood that he was dead and started to cry again, and then he disappeared.

The next morning at breakfast I told my mother what had happened, that Timmy had been killed. My mother said that she had told me that the night before Timmy had been run over on Islip Avenue, a heavily traveled street that had to be crossed to get to the fishing hole. But she was wrong. Timmy had been run over at around midnight, and I had gone to bed at about nine o'clock. I couldn't have known that unless he had appeared to me.

CROSSING OVER

As I grew up, I had more and more contact with the dead, and I got a little self-satisfied. I told myself that I had experienced them in every way possible. I had seen them in human and other forms, such as flashes of light, outlines in neon and mists, sounds and shadows, and just movement in my peripheral vision. I had received and sent messages to them and learned to not be terrified. I even grew to like them later in life, even grew to look forward to their visits because I knew that when they appeared they had something significant to say. But overall, I'm a little embarrassed to say that I had become desensitized to them to a large degree. I experienced the dead, ho-hum, so what else is new?

But life has a way of coming up and slapping you up side the head when you least expect it. So it was that I had such an experience. In brief, I died . . . and came back.

It all started in 1995 with a radio show I cohosted on WEVD, an AM station on Seventh Avenue in Manhattan. It was my first radio show, and it ran from ten to midnight on Saturdays. Our guests on the show included anyone involved with spiritual matter and the paranormal. My cohost, Mike Davis, would interview the guests who didn't have any direct experience in psychic matters, and I would interview those who did. We succeeded in getting some big names, such as Neale Donald Walsch, author of *Conversations with God;* Betty Eadie, author of *Embraced by the Light;* Brian Weiss, an expert on psychic matters; and Pat Morrison, the wife of Jim Morrison of The Doors. But one day our producer, Daryl McNicholas, announced that he thought he had really hit a home run. Dr. Raymond A. Moody was going to appear on the show.

I was thrilled. Dr. Moody is one of the great trailbreakers in the psychic field. Author of the phenomenal bestseller *Life After Life,* and the man who coined the phrase "near-death experience," Dr. Moody has helped many people reevaluate the whole psychic experience and to regard it as something legitimate. And make no mistake about it: Dr. Moody's book is groundbreaking and legitimate. *Life After Life* contains statements from over one hundred people who experienced clinical death (meaning that life-monitoring equipment showed no signs of life whatsoever) and came back. The awe-inspiring testimonies contained in his book show striking similarities. No matter what their circumstance, no matter what their age or gender, almost all of the one hundred people interviewed reported seeing a white light, a light so bright, so vivid, and so overwhelmingly positive that it took away their fear of the hereafter.

Many have told me that they felt that their lives were broadened and deepened by a near-death experience, that because of it they became more reflective and more concerned with ultimate philosophical issues.

—Dr. Raymond A. Moody

Reporting on this experience in *Life After Life,* Dr. Moody was able to reach far beyond the initial one hundred. He was able to pass along this life-affirming message to the ten million people who have read his book.

I had been a fan of Dr. Moody's for many years, so when the day came and this soft-spoken, scholarly man sat down in the WEVD studios I was overjoyed. To me, the most fascinating thing he brought up during the interview was the psychomanteum—also known as the Oracle of the Dead—in which people would "mirror gaze." The practice started with the ancient Greeks who would create some dark enclosure, then go inside it and gaze into a reflective surface such as a mirror or some highly shined brass pot. The surface was elevated so that the gazer could not make out his own image, but would see instead the image of a deceased loved one. Well, that was the hope.

Moody said that ancient reports indicated that many of the mirror gazers had been successful in seeing loved ones. For example, in the early fifties, an underground maze of tunnels was unearthed in Epirus, an area in Western Greece. Archeologists found a psychomanteum in one of them and the remnants of a huge bronze cauldron, which investigators calculated had been hung from a ceiling and into which mirror gazers looked. The massive side of the cauldron would have created huge, life-size apparitions, since the size of the vision is directly related to the size of the viewing surface.

Ancient Greek mirror gazers usually carried foodstuffs as gifts for the deceased, and would stay in the psychomanteum an astonishing thirty days. Tattered writings of one of the priests who oversaw the psychomanteum told the stories of those who had gazed. One of them, a young woman, had gone there to try to communicate with her husband, a soldier who had been killed in battle, and was successful. She cried out with "unabandoned joy" when he appeared.

Moody became interested in and then entranced by mirror gazing as a way of duplicating the near-death experience to help people who were grieving over lost loved ones. If he could bring the loved ones forth, it would have a very positive impact on the survivors, make them better able to deal with grief. He built a psychomanteum in his house and so far, as he reported in *Reunions:*

Visionary Encounters with Departed Loved Ones, of the ten people who had undergone the experience, half had had loved ones appear.

Moody had created his psychomanteum with a strictly visual goal in mind, that the dead would appear in the mirror. But in some cases the experience became auditory as well—the dead actually spoke. And in one startling case a woman's grandfather actually came out of the mirror to comfort her!

When Moody suggested that I might want to do some mirror gazing I took him up on it immediately. I wasn't looking to see anyone in particular. I just wanted to see what it would be like, if I really could see images of people who had passed. Little did I know that it would be one of the most profound experiences of my life.

So, we made arrangements and a couple of months later, on a lovely October day, I traveled down to the small town in rural Alabama where Moody lived. The house the doctor lived in was a converted gristmill next to a creek, a sprawling three-story home with a wraparound porch. It looked to be about a hundred years old. Inside, Moody had all the comforts of a fine old Southern home: beautifully carved and finished furniture, satiny wide-board wood floors with elegant trim, and among the many rooms, a kitchen that seemed large enough to park a horse and buggy.

I arrived in Alabama with my cohost and producer, who were also interested in mirror gazing. Moody gave us a tour of the place soon after our arrival, spending most of the time on the top floor, a windowless attic that had been remodeled into a finished room. It was in that room that Moody had installed the psychomanteum.

The psychomanteum was housed inside a large walk-in closet. It was simple, but cleverly designed. A 4-by-3½-foot mirror was positioned at one end of the closet, with the bottom edge of the mirror elevated some 3 feet above the floor. A comfortable easy chair with no legs and a slightly inclined backrest was located opposite the mirror at a distance of about 3 feet, and the only light was a single 15-watt lamp set behind the chair. The idea was that the subject would sit in the dark, positioned at such an angle that he could not see his reflection in the mirror, just the "crystal-clear pool of darkness" that Moody described in his book. Privacy was vital, of course, so the door remained closed.

Moody wanted to make sure the psychomanteum was safe. He had consulted with a number of the world's leading experts on apparitions of the deceased to make sure that people entering his psychomanteum would not be harmed by the experience in any way. None of the experts he spoke with believed it was dangerous.

I was to go into the chamber the day after I arrived. But before Dr. Moody would consent finally to my going into the psychomanteum, he insisted on asking me a number of questions to make sure that I was mentally stable. He asked me, among other things, if I had ever had any mental breakdowns, if I was being treated for a mental condition, and how I felt about the experience: Did I think I would be able to withstand it without any problems? My answers confirmed what I knew he knew: I was stable.

The next morning, my anticipation and enthusiasm for the experience building, I met Moody at ten o'clock. I was a little nervous, but intensely curious as to what would happen. I arrived wearing lightweight clothing and comfortable walking shoes as Dr. Moody had suggested. I was to go into the psychomanteum that afternoon, not because the experience required a special time, but because it was convenient. My colleagues had no roles in the procedure, so they went into town to go shopping with Moody's wife Cheryl.

I had a light caffeine-free breakfast and then Moody and I took a leisurely walk in the countryside. We talked about various things—my radio show, his practice, how he had gotten into mirror gazing (he had come across a book on it in an old bookstore), family matters—just a whole host of things which, I knew, were designed to depressurize someone who was nervous. He was also trying to show me that there was nothing to be afraid of. After all, if one of the best doctors of the paranormal wasn't worried about it, why should I be? It helped. The nervousness I felt drained off substantially.

After the walk we ate a lunch of soup, broiled fish, rice, and fruit juice. When we sat down and had another long talk it soon became clear that Moody was probing again. The last thing he wanted was for me to freak out during the experience.

When four o'clock came I was ready. At first I lay on a recliner outside the chamber listening to music to relax myself totally. Then, after twenty minutes or so, Moody led me into the chamber. I sat down in the armchair and tried to let go. All lights had been extinguished except the one behind me.

I looked up at the mirror. Just a shimmering rectangle of black glass.

I waited.

Nothing happened. No one was reflected in the mirror. No dead people. Nothing. I wondered if I had to wait a long time for someone to show up. The ancient Greeks stayed in the psychomanteum for thirty days—was I going to have to stay here a month? I tried to be patient. And then, suddenly, I became aware of an odd sensation. At first I felt like I was moving toward the mirror in my mind. And then I knew . . . I was entering through the dark glass which was no longer impenetrable. I was aware that I was walking forward, away from where I had entered, and I could make out the faint outlines of a U-shaped tunnel.

Looking back I suppose I should have been terrified. After all, I was in a black tunnel leading who knows where . . . but I wasn't afraid, just curious as to what lay ahead.

I walked through that tunnel for I don't know how long, and then . . . far, far ahead of me, I saw a pinpoint of light. As I approached, the pinpoint expanded to the size of a diamond, then a ball, and then it just started getting bigger and bigger and bigger. Streaks of light shot past me down the length of the tunnel and the tunnel started to become illuminated, as if someone were gradually turning the lights up. And then, abruptly, profoundly, I knew what it was. The light. The bright, vivid light of purity that Dr. Moody's respondents had talked about. *The* light beyond which was the world of Heaven, whatever that might be—Protestant, Catholic, Jewish, Muslim, Buddhist . . . whatever. I was walking toward the light and I felt good. Very, very, good.

I noticed that the temperature had changed. When I first passed into the tunnel it was cool, but it started getting warmer; not uncomfortably warm but pleasantly so, like a mild spring day. The tunnel kept getting lighter and lighter . . . and then it was lit like daylight, except there was a mist. And then I saw it. Up ahead and to my right, maybe fifteen yards away, movement. Then the movement got closer . . . and then it became human. There it was, a fully clothed human body. I say "body," but perhaps "human form" would be closer to the truth because it was headless . . . faceless . . . just large, expressive eyes in the proper position in terms of spacing, but not set into a face. It was like nothing I had ever seen before, and yet I knew who it was: a neighbor, an old man named Otto Schmidt. In life, Otto was bald and wore loud clothes, and that was the way he was dressed here. He had on green pants and a yellow, short-sleeved shirt. I was sure it was him. There was no mistaking those eyes.

Then other people started to appear, also without faces. Still, I recognized most of them. Neighbors, kids who had died when I was young, old people, aunts, and uncles. They filed by me on both sides, touching me, an army of the dead, but an army I was not afraid of, nor were they afraid of me. Those eyes looked at me with benevolence and love. They just seemed curious, friendly, very accepting. I saw my great grandmother Mary and I started to feel even better. Very, very good indeed. I knew I had died, but I didn't care. In fact I loved the idea because I knew that with each stride I was putting behind me all the heartache and sadness and fear of life. I was finally free.

I strolled along, getting closer to the main light, which got

---

We are not human-beings having a spiritual experience. We are spiritual-beings have a human experience.

—Pierre Teilhard de Chardin

---

brighter but did not hurt my eyes. I was almost there, very close to the brightest light of all and through which I would pass into the Heavenworld. Then, I felt something poking my back.

I stopped and glanced back and saw my great grandmother Mary looking up at me, her large eyes sad and concerned. And, just as she had done in my room, she spoke to me telepathically. Her message was clear and urgent.

"You have to go back, Jeffrey," she said, "you have to go back. Your wife and children need you. Go back!"

But I didn't *want* to go back. I didn't even know if I could. I just wanted to keep going to the light. And why go back, anyway? I knew that someday my wife and boys would join me. It was all so elementary. I hesitated, literally between life and death—no, a new life. . . . But some part of me knew that I could not go to the light. I could see my wife and two boys way, way back there, waiting for me, depending on me, loving me, needing me.

Oh God! I had to go back.

Reluctantly, very reluctantly, as if in slow motion, I turned and started walking back the way I had come, and as I did the light got dimmer, the mist started to disappear, the warmth faded and the tunnel became chilly. Some part of me was very sad, but I knew that I was doing the right thing. And as I walked, the people who passed me going in passed me going out, and I could feel the warmth, the thick sweetness of their approval.

I awoke on the chair in the psychomanteum, my clothing drenched with sweat, feeling weaker than a cat. I was sick. Very sick.

That night my temperature kept getting higher. I continued getting weaker and my gastrointestinal tract was in an uproar. In fact, I got so sick (I had a temperature of 104), that Moody was ready to put me in the hospital. But I resisted, and eventually I started to feel better.

Today, I have no doubt that my physical reaction was a response to having crossed over. I had not been prepared for crossing over. If I had known that was going to happen I would have grounded myself, mentally attached myself to a sort of bungee cord so I would be ready to pull myself back. And I have no doubt, either, that it was love that brought me back. The love of the dead for the living, and the love that was inside me for my family.

That experience confirmed for me just how loving the dead really are. I know my great grandmother was glad to see me, and so were all the other folks from my past. But love won. My great grandmother Mary knew that my wife and two boys had a need for me that was great, and while she wanted me with her, she cared more about my family than herself. I think of myself as a loving person, but I had a choice there too, and I was never so tempted in my life by anything like that. But it was an apple I chose not to bite into. Love was stronger.

One caveat. Please do not create your own psychomanteum or try to do this without competent, knowledgeable people in attendance. And if you want to do it, think it through: What are your motives? How far are you willing to go? Are you ready to take a one-way trip?

THE DEAD LOVE US

I had first started to notice the love and care the dead have for the living when I was a little boy. Remember Timmy, the kid who had been run over and appeared to me in lighted, neon-bulb outline the night he had been killed? I never really knew why Timmy had appeared, not at first anyway. But shortly after I saw him, something profoundly important had happened in my life. I met Joanie Lopez.

A friend of my mother's, Joanie was a tall, thin, dark-haired, dark-eyed woman who lived in one of the garden apartments near us. I was instantly fascinated by Joanie. I knew right away she was special. Joanie was a psychic, or a medium, as anyone who could do paranormal things in those days was characterized, and my mother allowed her to conduct what I later knew as "psychic parties" in our house. These psychic parties were something like Tupperware parties—only without the Tupperware. Ten or twelve people, almost always women, would come to our house for coffee, conversation, and psychic readings.

Joanie was kind to me. She took an active interest in mentoring me, and taught me many of the special things she knew. It was Joanie who talked to me about the responsibilities of being psychic, and it was Joanie who, soon after our first meeting, predicted that I would "some day do what she did," only I would do it on radio and TV.

One of the first things she taught me was about the love the dead have for the living. "When the dead appear," Joanie explained, "they want to help the living. Sometimes they want to alleviate pain, and sometimes they want to show us the best paths to take."

The bodies of the dead may die, but not their souls. And their souls are informed by love.

—Joanie Lopez

Then why, I asked her a few weeks after Timmy died, did he come to me? And why did he tell me he was dead, that I should not be afraid that he was "going to the light"? Joanie didn't feel she could answer my question specifically, but she did say that she believed it was because of love. I sensed she was right, but I couldn't explain it any further.

About a week later, I was back at the lake where Timmy used

to go. It was August and a normal day in every respect. The sun was out and though very warm, I didn't notice it much, particularly since I had my fishing line in the water and was eager for some curious catfish to try to make a dinner of the worm he saw. And then I saw Karen, Timmy's sister. A pretty, blonde girl of about fourteen—chubby like Timmy and very sweet—Karen was about 25 yards away standing at the edge of the lake.

I had seen Karen a number of times before (a number of times at the lake, in fact), but this time she looked a little strange. She didn't seem to be doing anything, just staring at the water. And she was sad. Of course, I thought. She was probably thinking about Timmy.

I felt compelled to go over to Karen and ask her how she was.

"Oh . . . I'm okay, Jeffrey," she said. "How are you?"

"I'm okay I guess."

And then—just like that—I understood why Timmy had come to me. I was his messenger. I had a message for Karen and her family.

"You know," I said, "I had a dream about Timmy."

"Really?" She seemed surprised. "When?"

I then described Timmy's appearance to me, and told Karen what I knew he wanted me to say.

"He wanted me to tell you all that he was all right. That he was going to the light. That God was going to take his hand and lead him into Heaven."

Karen had China-blue eyes, and she just looked at me a moment, then her eyes filled with tears.

"How can you be sure it was him?"

"He had his fishing pole with him."

She blinked, making tears stream down her cheeks.

"Thank you," she said. "Thank you."

And then she turned and left. I knew she was headed straight for her family. And I felt wonderful.

LIFESAVERS

More than anything the dead like to save lives. I've seen it happen many, many times.

Consider this. I was doing a psychic party in a house in Dix Hills, New York, and as usual, I was using one of the rooms in the house for individual readings. In this case, I was using the bedroom of the hostess' son, a young man named Richard. The procedure was always the same during my psychic parties. One by one, each of the people at the party would come into the room and sit down. Then I would do my reading, during which the particular person would then unload his or her problems, and I would provide whatever information I could based on all the various psychic energies that had come to me.

The procedure allowed me a few minutes' spare time between clients, and on this particular day, after my third consultation, I was sitting in a chair waiting for the next client to come in when I started to feel something I couldn't quite identify. But then the feeling became more pronounced, and I realized that I was feeling high, as if I was on drugs or alcohol. Then bad feelings started to seep into me. Feelings of sadness and despair and hopelessness. My eyes teared. I knew that I was experiencing someone else's feelings. I knew that person was in trouble.

Then a dead person appeared a few feet from where I was sitting. It was an old lady, in full human form, all dolled up, wearing plenty of rouge, lipstick, and mascara. Her ears and arms were glittering with what looked like expensive jewelry. I knew instantly that she was not here to talk about life in the hereafter. The dead never appear just to pass the time of day.

"My name is Grandma Sophie," she said. "Richard is one of my grandchildren."

I nodded hello.

"I'm worried," she said, "my Richard is taking drugs. He's addicted to them."

I let my energy cross telepathically with my question:

"What kind of drugs?"

"Cocaine," she said, "and what's more he's selling it to other people." She paused. "He's only twenty-two years old."

Her head dropped, and then she looked at me, her eyes full of sadness.

"If he doesn't stop," she said, "he's going to die."

Grandma Sophie communicated some potent details to me that spurred me into action. I went out of the room immediately and went up to Richard's mother, Anne, who was in the living room. I took her aside and told her that we had to talk—right away. She led me outside to the adjacent patio and shut the sliding glass door behind us.

"I have to tell you something," I said, "that Grandma Sophie told me. . . ."

"Grandma Sophie's dead," Anne said.

"I know. But listen to me."

I gave her the details. Then we went back into Richard's room and his mother immediately went to the bottom drawer of his dresser, where Grandma Sophie had told me to go. Anne found what cops call a "felony weight" package of powdered cocaine. If a cop would have come into Richard's room right then he would have been facing years in prison. Richard's mother was distraught.

"What am I going to do?" she asked.

"When is he coming home?"

"In an hour or so."

"I'll talk to him."

I continued the sessions, trying my best to concentrate, but I was distracted by my concern for Richard. When he came into the house two hours later, I was shocked to see how old and decrepit this young man looked. His eyes were watery and dilated. His nose was red and running. Except for some red blotches on his face, his complexion was chalky and gray. I wondered how anyone could not know that he was on drugs. Only someone who didn't want to know, I thought.

I got him aside in an empty room and laid into him.

"You know what I do, right?"

"Yeah," he said, "sure. You're the Swami."

"Well, Richard, one of the things I do is communicate with those who have passed to get a line on someone's future. Your Grandma Sophie appeared on your behalf. She told me that if you continue to go down the coke road you're on that you'll have no future. In fact she says she sees you in a coffin at Malden Mortuary."

This got his attention. The wise guy look disappeared from his face.

"She says she sees you in a mahogany coffin, surrounded by all kinds of beautiful flowers, and you're looking so bizarre, bizarre because you don't belong in a coffin at twenty-two years of age! And your mother and father are in the room and every now and then your mother cries. And you know your sister Vicki, the one who admires you so much?"

He nodded. My words were hitting him like a hammer in the gut.

"She can't cry. She's afraid to cry because she feels that once she starts she won't be able to stop."

We stood silently for a moment. Then he said, soft and low, and with great sadness, "I can't stop."

"Yes you can." I put my arms around this troubled young man and held him tight for a long time. "And you will."

I alerted Richard's mother on how she could do an intervention. She and her husband contacted a local drug counseling outfit, and they advised Richard's parents to commit him to South Oaks Hospital in Suffolk County, where he could get the kind of treatment he needed. Six months later I got a call from his mother.

"Richard has been out of the hospital for three months," she said. "He seems to be doing fine."

"Well," I said, "he will continue to do fine. I have that from no less an authority than Grandma Sophie."

Just because you get a message from a dead person, it doesn't mean that you can't stop it dead in its tracks . . .

There was a postscript to the story. Many years later I had a "chance" encounter with Richard. He was walking in Roosevelt Field Mall in Long Island with a very pretty woman. He looked terrific. In fact, he looked so good that I almost didn't recognize him. His eyes and skin were clear, and he just exuded contentment. I stopped him.

"I can't thank you enough," he said. And again I gave him my standard answer, where only the names have changed.

"Thank Grandma Sophie," I said.

DÉJÀ VU

- Understanding the dead is vital to developing your psychic potential.
- The psychomanteum is an ancient Greek device for seeing the dead. By gazing in a mirror in a darkened area you can see them appear in the mirror. *Do not* attempt to use a psychomanteum without getting professional advice.
- The dead have the same personalities in death as they do in life, but as time goes by they evolve, shedding negative characteristics. In essence, they become better spirits.
- The dead always tell the truth and they always come back to help the living, particularly to save lives.
- The dead tell you what is true, and also what is going to happen. But that doesn't mean that you can't change the blueprint of your life to avoid something undesirable.
- The dead may appear as a light, a flash, or orb—and also in full human form. Why they choose one form over another is a mystery. For now . . .

FOUR

The Language of the Dead

FOLLOWING FORM

I am by nature introspective. I'm always thinking about things in one way or another, and when I was in junior year of high school I started to really give some serious thought to the dead, to consider why they appeared in certain forms, and how they could best be understood. Why did my friend Timmy show up in neon while my great grandmother Mary appeared in full human form? Why do some dead people appear as a dream, or as a flash, a mist, or a sound? Why not just walk up in full body, fully dressed, as they of course sometimes appear?

I've thought about it long and hard and finally reached a conclusion of sorts. Form follows energy. It's the energy that gives life to the form—in this case the energy of the dead—and it's the energy that we're reading. Some of us are able to see this energy only in its most rudimentary of forms, such as dreams. Others who have more finely developed psychic instincts will be able to see more complex forms of energy such as orbs, light forms, and full-body appearances. In fact, not only will those with more finely developed psychic abilities be able to see this energy, but they'll be able to understand it better, and in some cases, to call upon it at will.

But the question remains: Why does this energy come in one form and not another? I believe that the dead appear in the form that we can best deal with. When my great grandmother Mary appeared to me I was very young. I didn't have a lot of the defenses that we put up as we get older, so I was open and curious. Plus—and I think this is important—I didn't know who Mary was. I didn't have any emotions invested in a relationship with her, so I was able to take her as is. That, I believe, made it easier for me to receive her. Yet, when I was a little older and Timmy came to me, he appeared in neon outline because he understood that I would have been very upset by a visit in full human form. I knew Timmy very well, remember. He was my good friend and news of his passing was very upsetting to me. I don't think I could have accepted the news in such an "in your face" kind of way. Chances are Timmy knew that. Hence the neon.

Full-Body Form

First I should say that while I am a psychic intuitive, I am *not* a geographer. I can get lost—and do. Well, one day when I was driving upstate near Albany, New York, I got myself onto a one-lane blacktop in the middle of nowhere. It was dusk of a cold day, and I was low on gas.

After just a few minutes of wondering which way to go, I saw someone walking up the road toward me. He approached me with a big smile on his face. I got good vibes from this unknown man, except he was strangely dressed—that is, his clothing seemed out of date. He wore heavy pants, boots, a big coat, and one of those brimmed caps that used to be popular in the thirties.

I asked the man if he knew how to get back on the main road. "Drive straight, turn left, and then go past the James farm," he said. "The main road is the next one beyond that."

I thanked him. He looked at me and smiled warmly and said: "I'm William James."

I followed Mr. James's directions and was happy to see, after I made the turn, a gas station. I stopped to fill up. As the gas station attendant pumped the gas into my car I figured I'd confirm the directions. I said that I had been told that the main road was just beyond the James farm down the road. The attendant looked at me strangely, wrinkling his brow.

"The James farm?" he said. "That's the *Donelly* farm. That place changed hands years ago. Sixty years ago in fact."

"There's no William James?"

The attendant looked quizzically at me.

"Well, there was. William James died forty years ago."

All souls were created in the beginning and are finding their way back to whence they came.

—Edgar Cayce

I recall another full-body visitation. I was about sixteen at the time, and my hormones were raging like the Colorado River. My girlfriend Bridget and I were alone in the house and had settled on the couch for some "smoochy coochie." Things were heating up when—goodness knows why—I looked over Bridget's shoulder and there, standing not three feet away, were two military figures: one in a World War II German uniform and the other in a French uniform.

Neither soldier "spoke" to me, nevertheless there was only one way to interpret this appearance: Take your hands off that young woman!

As soon as I disentangled myself the soldiers disappeared.

Later, I found out that one of the men was Bridget's great grandfather on her mother's side, the other a grandfather on her father's side. Why had they appeared in full-body form? Well, I was a sixteen-year-old boy and pretty excited. I think the only thing that could have interrupted me was the army!

Light Forms

Helen Duffy was telling me of her experience "seeing a flash of light" out of the corner of her eye:

"I was standing in the kitchen," she said, "when I looked past the dining room to the base of the stairs which led to the second floor. I got a very clear image of my father going up the stairs. He looked like he did when he died: white haired and thin. He was carrying a box full of plumbing tools. I could see some pipe sticking out at one end of the box.

"It didn't take me long to figure out his message. I had been considering whether or not to have a new bath added to the second floor, and if my father were alive he would have been handy enough to do it. But the fact that he was going up the stairs with the tools meant he approved of me getting it done. More important than that, though, I now understand that he's with me."

Helen had experienced a "light form" visitation from her father. Light forms are manifestations of energy from people who have passed. Some light forms appear simply as bursts, flashes, and streaks, and even mists and shadows. (I include mists and shadows in this category because even though, strictly speaking, they are not light, they do act in the same way.) Not all light forms contain a physical image as Helen had experienced. Sometimes there will be an image following the light flash, but as often as not there will be just a feeling that comes with the light, such as the felling you get when a bird flies by.

I remember the time I was on a 727 that was approaching JFK International Airport when, all of a sudden, something flashed out of the side of my eye. For a moment I thought it was sunlight reflected off the wing, but the feeling that followed told me that the experience was psychic, even though there was no visual image or other physical manifestation. You see, I was worried about my friend, Jack Lucas. We hadn't seen each other for a while, but he was distinctly on my mind. I couldn't shake the thought of him.

I decided to visit Jack, who lived in a quaint house in Valley Stream, Long Island. I was worried, but not sure why. I had a hard time focusing on the drive to Jack's house, and when I arrived, I kept getting this terrible fear of him being in the hospital. I got out of the car, went to the house, and when Jack opened the door . . . I was shocked. His skin was dull yellow. His eyes were pale and it looked like he had lost a lot of weight. Jack worked nights at different nightclubs around the city where bad lighting is the norm, so it wasn't surprising that I was the first to tell him how bad he looked. I asked him how he was feeling. "Not good," he said predictably. As gently as I could, I told him of my fear, and an hour later we were sitting in the emergency ward of a local hospital. Jack was hospitalized for a few days, and I'm happy to say that he's doing fine.

Was it the flash of light that gave me the premonition about Jack? You bet!

Talk to Me

Light form and human form appearances are visual. But not all visitations are. Sometimes the dead "speak" telepathically by transferring energy from their being to our sixth sense. Sometimes the information contained in this telepathic language is plain and easy-to-understand, as direct as a message can be. That's what happened to my client Anne Renjillian. When she received an appearance by her beloved grandmother there was no mistaking the message: "The man you are going out with is not a good man. Lewis will hurt you. Get away from him."

The dead don't lie. What's more, they can look down a corridor of time that living people can't. I suggested Anne follow her grandmother's advice, which she did immediately. Good thing too, because as Anne and I were both to learn, the "clean upstanding citizen" she had known as Lewis was actually a drug dealer with a criminal record.

It's rare that a message from the dead will be this direct though. More likely than not the communication will be symbolic and will require much more work on our part to decipher. For some impenetrable reason—at least impenetrable to me—the dead don't like to communicate in plain English. They seem to prefer riddles and symbolic language much more. The problem with this is that we mere mortals must interpret the symbols, assemble the pieces of the puzzle, and decipher the message. And that's not always easy.

Behold, a sacred voice is calling you. All over the sky a sacred voice is calling.

—Black Elk

It might help to think of interpreting the symbolic language of the dead in the same way as you think of interpreting a dream. For example in a dream you may think about the planet Mars, then picture a man riding a very fast bike, and then be scared by a fire. And the real meaning of the dream could be that you don't want your son, Marty, who is represented by the planet "Mars," buying a motorcycle, represented by the bike (which is the nickname of a motorcycle) because you're afraid he'll get into an accident and get killed in a flaming crash, which is symbolized by your fear of a fire.

A short while ago I had a visit from a woman named Jean Catalano, who came to tell me that her deceased father had shown up a few weeks earlier—speaking Italian. Now, Italian was Jean's father's first language, but he rarely used it around his daughter for the simple reason that she couldn't understand it. I don't speak Italian either, but I did ask Jean if she could repeat the words, which she did. I then called one of my psychic mentors Joanie Lopez, who speaks Spanish, to see if she could help. Jean and I were thrilled when Joanie was able to translate Mr. Catalano's words, but I've got to tell you that we were really baffled by the message itself: "I like your lemon tree. Arthur will too. He loves you."

So, we started to decipher the message. Did Jean have a lemon tree? No. Did she know someone called Arthur? No. Hmmm. So, what was the significance of the lemon tree? Certainly there weren't any in New York, where Jean lived. Did she have a vacation planned to somewhere hot, somewhere lemon trees grew? No again. What could it be? Then, just as we were about to give up: a revelation.

"The Lemon Tree," shouted Jean. "It's a chain of hairstylists! That's it. My dad is saying that he likes my hairstyle!?"

Jean was so excited I hated to correct her. "If you remember, Jean, it's Arthur who likes your hair. Or rather, he *will*."

A psychic can misinterpret a message from the dead, just as a psychiatrist can misinterpret a dream.

It's important to pay attention to the exact wording of messages. If we can remember them, that is. Mr. Catalano's message said that Arthur *will* like your hair. Future tense. That told us that Arthur was someone that Jean didn't know yet, but would. So, now we were able to put the pieces of the message together. Jean was going to meet someone called Arthur who was going to like her hair. Since liking a woman's hair seems personal, we figured that this Arthur was going to be a romantic involvement for Jean. An important one at that. We were right! Eleven months later Jean met a man named Arthur Spagnoli . . . who complimented her on her hair. After a whirlwind courtship, Jean and Arthur were married.

It takes practice to put these pieces together. And bear in mind that nobody is right all the time. A psychic can misinterpret a message from the dead, just as a psychiatrist can misinterpret a dream. Symbols are intrinsically ambiguous, and it is sometimes very difficult to nail down the exact meaning of a communication. To give you an example, I remember reading one client who had a dead person appear with a rose in his lapel. I figured it was a slam dunk because the client's mother's name was "Rose," and all I had to do was relate everything to her. Fine. Except it had nothing to do with her. The information given was about a career move for a young man in the family—he "rose" to success.

AN EXPANSIVE VIEW

Keep in mind that the spirits love us. Also keep in mind that they have a more expansive view of things than we do, so sometimes they'll give us what we need, not necessarily what we want. I know this sounds like the psychic equivalent of eating your vegetables, but you've just got to trust me on this.

Sometimes when we try to contact the spirit world we'll ask one person to show up and in fact quite a different person will appear. That happens to me all the time. I ask for a mother, I get a father. I ask for a father, I get a sister. I ask for a brother, I get a cousin. I ask for this person or that person and sometimes a complete stranger or group of strangers shows up.

Just this morning I did a reading for a woman who, like so many of my clients, came to find out if a loved one was okay. In Sara's case it was her father, who had died a slow, lingering death that had been painful for him and also for the people who had to watch him die.

I tried to reach across to connect with Sara's father, get him to appear, but a woman appeared instead. I didn't know what any of Sara's relatives looked like, if indeed this was a relative, so I described the woman to Sara, telling her that she was a beautiful blonde about thirty years old. The woman was wearing an old-fashioned pleated white dress, and though the dress was loose fitting, it was very clear that she had a shapely figure. She also had on a necklace with beads that alternated between green and black. The woman was a vision of loveliness, but there was one thing that seemed very out of place. The woman was cradling a small, beautiful statuette made of some sort of polished white stone, and occasionally she would look down on it, lovingly I thought.

"The statuette," I said, "it looks as if it's of a bearded man, and he's holding a hammer. Does this mean anything to you?"

Sara shook her head. I tried to probe into my own mind to determine the meaning. I just let myself go, relaxing even more than I already was (a requirement for connecting psychically), and waited for an answer. But there was no answer. The figure that had come across merely looked at me, holding the statuette in that loving, affectionate way.

I wasn't able to get anything from her that would be helpful to Sara and I was about to take another tack when Sara blurted out:

"Oh my God," she said, "oh my God. I think I know who that is . . ."

I was silent.

"That's my grandmother, Winnie. She died when my father was very young but I remember seeing a picture of her a long time ago. It was a black and white picture but she had on a beaded necklace that I think is what you're seeing. My father was raised by an aunt."

Something clicked in my mind.

"Is your father's name Joseph?"

"Yes," Sara said, "how did you know?"

"The statue. I think it's a statue of St. Joseph. It's Jesus' father and he was a carpenter. Your father is with your mother. He's in her care now. He's the statuette, her baby, her child."

Sara started to sob.

"Oh yes," she said, "oh yes. He's with her now. He's okay?"

"Yes," I said, "what could be better than to be with his mother? He's gone home to her after all these years."

Remember: The spirits love us. It's as simple as that.

Don't be surprised if you get a message delivered by someone you're not familiar with at all. That's what happened to me early in my career when I was doing another psychic party, this time out in Bellerose, New Jersey where a group of grade school teachers had gathered.

It was a long drive from Queens to Bellerose, so by the time I got there in my rattletrap, kidney-knocking old Chevy I had to hit the bathroom. Fast. I finished my business and was washing my hands when I saw a pale orange light flash out of the side of my eye. I had a visitor. Whoever it was didn't stick around. Still, some images formed in my head, a picture of an eleven-year-old girl called "Nicole" or "Nicky" or "Nancy"—some name beginning with the letter *N*. Suddenly I felt very depressed. A moment later I knew why. I saw this little girl with the *N* name in this very bathroom, six days from the day, cutting her wrists deeply with a razor blade. I saw this little girl dying on the floor, her blood a vivid red pool against the stark white floor. Another image told me to check for a suicide note under her underwear in a dresser in the little girl's bedroom. I was horrified. By the time I got outside I was shaking. I went up to the lady, Janisce, who arranged the party and asked her if she had a young daughter whose name began with the letter *N*.

"Yes," she said. "That's my daughter Noreen."

As gently as I could I told her what I had seen.

"How do you know for sure?"

I told her about the note. We went into Noreen's room and when she came out she was ashen . . . and her shaking hands were holding a note.

"I hate him! I hate him!" it read.

The woman and her husband immediately sought out psychiatric assistance, which in short order resulted in the unearthing of Noreen's problem: an on-going molestation by one of her teachers, who was subsequently arrested and given jail time. The last I had heard of Noreen was that she was continuing to see the psychiatrist on a regular basis. I didn't know for quite a while how she turned out until years later when I was having a particularly difficult day in my office.

The phone rang. I picked up and heard a woman's voice. It was Noreen. She was still a bit haunted by what happened, but was one hundred times better than it had been when she was a little girl.

"I wanted to thank you," she said, "so, so much."

The most difficult thing in life is to know yourself.

—Thales

"Hey," I said, "just hearing your voice is thanks enough."

Sometimes the people you want to contact show up, but they don't have the answers you're seeking, as my friend Tommy Panzini found out. Tommy operates a music store in Long Island and is a professional singer. About ten years ago, he came to me looking for some answers about a romantic relationship in which he was involved. I told him I'd see what I could do. Tommy was intent on becoming engaged to a certain young woman, but when his father told me that it wasn't going to happen, that she wasn't the right girl and would end up hurting him, he was really disappointed. Then two other loved ones appeared—an aunt and uncle of his—and they had other advice, but not about his love life.

Tommy was very irritated. Skeptical by nature, he was a little miffed by the response I gave him, and seemed even more annoyed by the information imparted by his aunt and uncle.

"Your aunt and uncle," I proceeded to tell Tommy, "say that your business is going to go through the roof! That your volume is going to quintuple in five years."

Still reeling from the disappointing news about his love life, Tommy was in no mood for business predictions, no matter how positive.

"How could that be," he said, "I have a little music store in New Hyde Park. How am I going to go through the roof?"

"I don't know," I said, "but that's what they're telling me."

As it turned out Tommy's business did go though the roof because he was able to sell his records, CD's, etc. worldwide through this new thing called "the Internet."

Oh . . . and do I need to tell you that Tommy is no longer a skeptic?

DÉJÀ VU

- The language of the dead doesn't have any absolute rules—it's not like English or Spanish—nevertheless, we can make some generalizations that can really help us in our efforts to communicate with those who have passed.
- The dead manifest themselves in various ways including forms of light, mists, and shadows. These are normally followed by a clear image and it's the image that carries the psychic information.
- The dead prefer speaking in symbols rather than plain language. Symbolic language requires more work on our part. It's important to pay attention to the message, to learn how to interpret the symbols, assemble the pieces, and decipher the message.
- The dead aren't always concerned with serious matters. Sometimes they help the living in matters that do not seem all that important in the scheme of things, so don't be surprised if you encounter them in entirely ordinary situations.
- When a dead person appears, it may not be the person you asked to see. Moreover, the dead do not necessarily answer your questions. They tell you what they want to.

FIVE

Sign Language

SIGNS

The dead like to leave signs, little indicators that show us they're still around. A sign might be a smell—a favorite perfume, for example, or a certain brand of cigar. It might be a sound, a change in temperature (ever felt a sudden chill?), or some mundane cue that will somehow cause us to make a connection with a person who has passed. Sometimes these signs contain messages, warnings, or encouragement—but more often than not they're just loving communications from those who have passed, like a Hallmark card from the spirit world.

The Nose Knows

Smells may be the most common indicator of a dead person's presence. These smells can come from anywhere, can be of anything, just so long as they can be clearly linked to a loved one who has passed. Cigarettes (*very* common), aftershave, the smell of freshly cut grass, or the aroma of a favorite food—the possibilities are really quite limitless. It's the link to the dead person that's key.

Usually these smells are not subtle. When you enter a room where a spirit resides, the smell will be strong and will suffuse the area in most, but not all, cases. Like other signs, the smell is intermittent, so you won't experience it all the time. One minute you think you smell cigarette smoke, then it will be gone, only to return again.

Trust your senses. If you think you've smelled something significant, chances are you have.

Of course it would be unusual for a house not to harbor the particular smell of one of its inhabitants. If a person lived in a house for thirty years and worked as a chef, say, or as a printer (or some other occupation where he came home with a lingering scent on his clothing), the smell would naturally be evident in the house even after he had passed. But remember, smells that are signs are intermittent, they come and go. They're different from the scents that linger after a person's death.

Don't be fooled into thinking that a smell will always be the aroma of something pleasant. Sometimes these odors can be very disagreeable. One person who came in for a reading told me that both she and her husband hated the particular brand of malodorous cigar her father smoked. She told me: "It took all our love to tolerate Papa smoking those dang cigars. They smelled like an outhouse!" Now, of course, she looks forward to the smell. "When I smell those darn things I know that Papa is around. That's fine with me."

Once I was asked to visit the home of two sisters who lived in New Jersey. They were sure their deceased father was making appearances.

"We smell him," one of the sisters said. "Our father was usually a fastidious man, but in the winter he tended to postpone his showers a day or so because he didn't want to endure the chill in the bathroom. Occasionally, well, um, occasionally he had body odor, and that's what we're smelling now."

"How long ago has he been gone?" I asked. I wanted to make sure that the sisters weren't actually smelling the lingering scent of their father. No chance of that.

"It will be eleven years this November," one of the sisters said.

Two days later I arrived at the house. I knew there was no guarantee that I'd be able to confirm that their father was around—the intermittent nature of appearances makes them impossible to rely on—still, I said I'd give it a try.

The sisters and I shared a few pleasantries before I went to an upstairs bathroom where they said they had detected his odor. I smelled nothing. I didn't give up, though. The dead move. That might be the case here.

There was no odor anywhere upstairs, including the attic, so I went back downstairs. Paydirt! One of the downstairs bedrooms was ripe with body odor that was, as the sisters suggested, a little offensive. The women were ecstatic by this confirmation from an impartial source. They couldn't have been more pleased.

Before I left I asked the ladies why their father's presence was so important to them. "We miss him so badly," one of the sisters said. "He was a wonderful father and a great man. It makes us feel better to know that he's still around."

Out in the Cold

Often when the dead are coming through from the other world they are accompanied by a sudden chill or coldness that comes from the convergence of differing energies. Spirits draw and retain energy from their immediate vicinity. The more energy the spirit can absorb the higher the potential for a communicative event. Sometimes a spirit may choose (or attempt) to manifest itself in such a way as to require a severe amount of energy. This can cause the immediate vicinity to be drained of energy, resulting in a sudden chill. Witness what happened one August day a few years ago, when the temperature was soaring past ninety and I got a call from a friend.

"A friend of mine has a 'feeling' that her dead mother is in her house. Could you come and check it out?"

It took me about a week before I had any time to visit this woman, a week during which the temperature continued to climb steadily. I was grateful the house had air-conditioning. The lady who had called me said that her mother had passed about six months earlier, and that her own feeling of her mom's presence had started about a week ago.

I conducted a standard investigation upstairs, going from room to room to determine if any spirits were present. I sensed nothing until I was pulled to a downstairs room, a master bedroom at one end of the house. The door to the bedroom was closed. I opened it, stepped inside . . . and was astonished by a fierce winter cold. In fact, it was so cold that I could see my breath! I checked the air-conditioning setting: 70 degrees. Just what I thought. The coldness was a sign from her mother.

"You're right," I said, "your mother has come back. And she's in her bedroom right now."

Hear That?

So often when we think about sounds associated with our loved ones we think about speech and forget the other incidental sounds that we make when going about our daily lives. Some people continually clear their throats, for example. Others may whistle, crack their knuckles, or scuff their shoes on the pavement. One person may associate the crisp turning of newspaper pages with her father, while another can't hear the song "Swanee River" without feeling close to her mother.

I had one client who used to hear a very ordinary sound that, under the circumstances, was very scary to her. This client would be asleep in bed on the second floor of her house and would awaken to the sound of a downstairs toilet flushing. Why so scary? This woman lived alone. She thought it might be a sign from her husband, who had died two years previously and had used the downstairs toilet constantly during the latter days of his illness.

"The first time I heard the sound," she said, "it bothered me, but when I heard it again on two separate nights it really scared me."

Just to be sure there was nothing wrong with the toilet, the woman called in a plumber. "I had heard that toilets can flush by themselves," she said.

Eighty-five dollars later the plumber pronounced the toilet in

---

Becky told me that she continually heard a meowing sound in her house, and it wasn't hard to determine that it was a sign from her mother, with the cat her mouthpiece. Becky's mother had owned an Abyssinian cat that lived to the ripe old age of twenty-one. When her mother died it wasn't long before the cat died too. But now, even though there are no animals in the house, Becky can occasionally hear the distinctive "Meow!" of her mother's cat. "It's very reassuring," she said.

---

good working order. When it flushed again in the middle of the night, the woman knew it was her husband.

Unusual Signs

Signs come and go, and of course they vary widely. There's really no limit to their variety. The key is to be tuned in to the possibilities of signs and to appreciate their random nature.

One day I was sitting in my office with a client who was terrified of flying. Richard had always avoided air travel—he would never vacation anywhere he couldn't drive—but now he had to attend a business conference three states away. Richard knew that missing the conference would mean jeopardizing his position in the company, so he came to see me for help in conquering his problem. Or at least coping with it.

"I break out in a sweat just driving to the airport," Richard confided. "The thought of flying brings me to my knees. It just doesn't seem natural to me to be up there like that. I don't know how *not* to be terrified."

Richard took a deep breath and tried to continue, but suddenly, as if seized by something outside of himself, he stopped in mid-sentence and looked out the window. The room was quiet for a moment, and just then a white bird landed on the branch of a tree outside. It was a beautiful white bird, not a seagull or a pigeon, and certainly not the sort of bird you see during a Long Island winter. Richard and I looked at each other in surprise.

"You know what that was, don't you?" I asked the client.

"No."

"That bird was a sign from your spirit guide. He's telling you that your flight is safe—100 percent safe. He wants you to know that it's all right. That everything will be okay."

It took some convincing for Richard to accept what I was saying, but the sight of that bird was so startling, the timing of it so perfect, that finally he gave up his resistance. Two weeks later Richard took his flight. Safe and sound just like his spirit guide told him.

Signs can be obvious—or sneaky. For example, one Saturday morning when I was getting dressed to go to the office, I turned on the TV, something I never do. A&E's *Biography* was showing, and this particular program was about John Wayne. I didn't watch much of the show (I was, after all, trying to get ready for work), but the part I did catch was about *Big Jake*, a movie that The Duke made in 1971 featuring a man called, you guessed it, Big Jake, and his grandson called Little Jake.

I suspected immediately that the name "Jake" had special significance, but I didn't know who it related to, or why.

**There are only two ways to live your life.
One is as though nothing is a miracle.
The other is as though everything is a
miracle.**

—Albert Einstein

My first client that morning was a woman who had lost her son in a car accident, and when I saw her everything became clear.

"Your son's name is Jake, isn't it?"

The blood drained from her face.

"How did you know?"

I told her that her Jake's psychic energy was passing through John Wayne's Big Jake character, and that her son was telling her that he was still around and doing okay. Was Jake in cahoots with the cable company? Not really . . . but he summoned me to turn on the TV, and trusted that I would take it from there. I told you they could be sneaky!

One client I had, Lucille Selg of Long Island, had a sign from her mother . . . in the form of a house fly. It sounds a little crazy, and maybe it is. But it happened.

The unusually large fly had first shown up in November, a strange time for a fly to be around in Long Island. It's cold on "The Island" in November and flies show up when it's warm.

I'm not kidding, but this fly got itself involved in all kinds of

---

Signs can assume some *very* interesting forms.

---

family business before they realized it was coming as a representative of Lucille's mother, who had died a few years earlier at the age of fifty-seven.

Lucille told me that one Sunday morning her father came to the house with a bag of bagels, including a plain bagel for munching on by her five-month-old daughter.

"I said, 'Dad, why do you want to give a little baby a bagel? She could bite off a piece of it and choke.'

"And then I said to him: 'If mother was here, she'd smack you in the head.'

"Almost immediately, that big fat housefly flew smack into my father's forehead. My father tried to shoo it away, but it was stubborn, not the kind of fly that shoos easily. It just paraded around the table.

"From that moment on," Lucille continued, "everywhere the baby was placed in the house the fly showed up. It hung around for weeks. I know it sounds strange, but I just knew it had something to do with my mother.

"Well, one day my father had enough of the fly, cupped it in his hands and opened the window, placed it on the sill, and closed the window behind it.

"The very next day it showed up! There was no way for it to get inside the house, but it did. The dang thing just mysteriously reappeared!

"The fly also got involved in the relationship my father had with a woman he had started to go out with named Rhia. She and that fly definitely didn't get along. One afternoon, for example, we were all at the dinner table—me and my brothers, my husband and my father and his new girlfriend—when suddenly this fly landed on the table between my father and Rhia. By then the kids sort of thought of the fly as being their grandma and they blurted out: '*Grandma!*' Well, that really pissed Rhia off and she tried to swat it. She missed it though, and it flew away right into her cup of coffee!

"This still didn't kill it, though, because I took the cup over to the sink and poured it out, first placing a napkin over the drain. Eventually the fly revived and flew away!"

As persistent as the fly was, I didn't believe that it was there just to be a buzzing nuisance. I told Lucille that her mother, as personified in the fly, was there just to let everyone know that she was around, that she actually was happy that her husband had started to go out with someone else. The last I heard Rhia was still going out with Lucille's father. More power to them.

Oh. One other thing about that fly. It lived for about three months, a good bit longer than the regular twenty-one-day life cycle of a fly. I have no problem believing in the validity of that fly. I really believe, as does Lucille, that the fly was infused with the energy of her mother. It was a very special fly indeed.

VALIDATION

Some signs don't have to be validated because they are so distinctive and overwhelming, readily understood by those who are open to the possibilities of the psychic world. Consider the following:

- rotten egg smells usually signify something pretty dreadful, such as sickness or death, even murder;
- perfume is usually a harbinger of some positive news;
- the aroma of flowers can indicate that a loved one is sending a congratulatory message on a special occasion such as a birthday or anniversary;
- a musty, stagnant aroma can signal the presence of an earthbound soul who is not at rest;
- a favorite song means *I'm thinking about you;*
- finding pennies signifies a visitor;
- electricity jolts, such as flickering or burnt-out light bulbs can indicate the presence of someone who has passed.

Not all signs can be so readily interpreted, though. Many aren't strong enough in themselves and they need to be validated, by which I mean there should be a confirming or second sign that the initial sign is actually from a spirit. Consider the example of an elderly woman named Ellen Cols who came into my Port Washington office a few years back. She was distraught, explaining that her husband, Ray, to whom she had been married for forty-eight years, had recently died. Ellen felt terribly alone. Frightened. All she could think of was communicating with him in one way or another. She had to know that he was okay.

Sometimes it's not possible to bring a dead person forward. Perhaps the dead person doesn't want to appear, or maybe the psychic energy channels are not as open as they could be. That's what happened in this case. Ellen's husband Ray did not come forward and I was unable to report to her how he was doing. So I told her that she should be alert to a sign from him, that he might choose a less direct way to communicate.

"What do you mean?"

"Well, sometimes the deceased give us a sign that their spirits are around."

"Like what?"

"Just things that you would normally associate with him like a smell, perhaps, a sound or a song. Anything, just as long as you clearly associate it with him. But be sensitive to what's going on around you because chances are that if he is going to appear he will do so shortly. People who have passed usually show up quite soon after they've crossed over."

"Okay."

I paused. Many times signs appear and people don't see them. Or more accurately, they see them but are not aware that they are signs.

"Can you recall any sign you may have received from him?"

"No, not that I'm aware of."

"Well, think a minute."

She did, but shook her head no.

Ellen left my office, but less than two hours later called me, ecstatic.

"On the way home," she said, "I heard a song on the radio. 'Auf Wiedersehen, Sweetheart.' I haven't heard it for years, maybe twenty years! But it was our favorite song and goes back to when we were courting."

"Great," I said, thrilled at how happy and encouraged Ellen was by the sign. Now you know I don't believe in coincidence, still, I thought that after the initial shock of the communication wore off Ellen might try to rationalize it in her mind. I wanted her to be sure, to really know in her heart that she had received a sign from her husband. "Be on the lookout," I counseled. "See if something else shows up that is related to Ray. I'd be surprised if it didn't."

"Okay," she said, still giddy. "I hope I call you soon."

The phone call came just two days later. Ellen was excited.

"I might have gotten a validation sign," she said. "Let me tell you what happened."

"Please."

"My husband was a great crossword puzzle freak," she said, "and so is one of my sons. Anyway, yesterday my son was doing *The Sunday Times* puzzle and he asked me for help with a certain question and the answer was . . . Oh Jeffrey . . . the answer was auf Wiedersehen!"

"Oh," I gasped, unable to contain myself.

"Do you *really* think that was a validation sign?"

"I do," I said. "I really do."

Then a pause.

"Jeffrey . . . ? "

"Yes, Ellen."

"You know why I'm so over the moon at Ray's choice of sign?"

"No," I responded, more than a little interested.

"Well . . . the last lines of the song . . ." she said in a suddenly calm and quiet voice, "the last lines of the song are 'With love that's true, I'll wait for you.' "

"Ohhhh," I said, choking back a tear.

"Do you think he's waiting Jeffrey?"

"Yes, Ellen. I really do."

Most of the time signs from the dead are simple to see, particularly when you are attuned to spotting them. You'll get a strong smell, or a very individualistic sound. Maybe a room will be very chilly, or you'll get two songs in a row that the deceased person liked. Or maybe a favorite movie will come on, followed by an-

---

I am not resigned to the shutting away of loving hearts in the hard ground.

—Edna St. Vincent Millay

---

other, and maybe even another. Your father's alma mater, a very small college that's hardly known to anyone, might come into the news and then a couple of days later the college will again come up, but this time in a completely different context, such as a new business with the very same name. Those are easy ones.

Sometimes, however, the signs are difficult to see and interpret, discernable once you've been doing this kind of stuff a long time. I had one client named Maria Alonso, for example, who lost her husband in a car accident. One day she was exiting a building when feathers started fluttering down from the sky out of nowhere. The feathers might have been a sign, or maybe not. Nevertheless when I think about feathers one thing comes to mind: angels. What better sign than that?

An even more difficult interpretation was required by a client named Jean Dunphy who came to me after her father, Hugh, had passed. Hugh had willed his car to his daughter. A 1998 Cadillac, a sleek blue car in mint condition, this car was his prize possession. Well, to honor her father's memory, Jean vowed to really look after the car, to care for it as her father had done. That meant cleaning it, inside and out.

One day while vacuuming the upholstery, Jean found a silver dollar under the driver's side seat. This would have meant nothing, she said, except that her father kept the car in impeccable condition. A CPA and highly astute money manager who was meticulous down to every last detail, Jean's father was *always* cleaning the car, which was why Jean was beside herself when she came to see me with the silver dollar she had found. Even if he had dropped it inadvertently, he never would have missed it during his frequent cleaning sessions. Jean was perplexed, and I have to admit, I was too; I couldn't give my client the interpretation she was asking for—the sign was far too ambiguous for me to understand—so I advised her to wait for another sign.

A couple of weeks later Jean was walking inside a shopping mall when she noticed a crumpled up piece of paper in a corner. Feeling compelled, she picked it up and unfolded it, discovering a dollar bill. When Jean told me about this at our next session it seemed to me that she or her family would be coming into money. But the more I thought about it psychically, the less inclined I was to accept that. In other words, my psychic sense of what was to be was not fully satisfied. So I gave it some thought. Obviously, her father was trying to give her some sort of sign that involved money. He was, after all, an accountant and a very fastidious man. So if he wasn't trying to tell Jean that she was going to come into some money, what could it be? Of course! I thought. The opposite. Jean wasn't going to find money. She was going to lose it! Only then did I feel satisfied. Only then did my intuitive voice calm down.

I called Jean and told her of my interpretation. As it happened, six months earlier she had invested almost thirteen thousand dollars in a risky stock offering. Since that was the only area in which she thought she could lose any money, Jean decided to sell the stock—for a slight profit. Not long after, the price of the

---

Sometimes signs can go unnoticed or are misinterpreted. And sometimes the consequences of this are tragic.

---

stock plummeted. So, as it turned out, the silver her father had left was worth not a dollar, but thirteen thousand!

One of the most horrific things I have ever been involved in had three separate signs, or warnings. I wish to God I was at the scene and available to try to interpret their meaning. Could I have stopped the resulting tragedy? Or was the die cast? I can't recall the event without a grinding feeling deep in my gut, a sadness passing across my heart that sometimes brings tears to my eyes.

It all started when I did a reading for a pretty young woman I'll call Carmen. During the reading I told Carmen that I saw a bad car accident involving her brother, and that the accident would transform a potentially wonderful day into one of sadness and mourning. Carmen couldn't connect it to any upcoming event, and neither could I, so unfortunately it quickly faded from view.

Around seven months later, her first cousin, not her brother—I misread that—a handsome young guy named Michael, got married in a lovely Catholic church in Lido Beach, Long Island, a town on the south shore of Long Island not too far from the Atlantic Ocean. When the wedding party exited the church there was the usual throng of well-wishers who happily pelted them with rice, took photos, and offered their congratulations. But something was odd. A number of the people were holding helium-filled balloons, but instead of rising, straining upward to be free as such balloons do, they were barely afloat, just a few feet off the ground.

How I wish I had been there. My interpretation would have been that that was a sign that the dead were around, that there was something to fear. The balloons were a warning. I would have immediately started to look for further validation, some other changes in the event that were not planned. As it happened, I would have seen them shortly.

The reception was to follow immediately and the guests loaded into limousines and cars . . . except two of the flower girls, who chose not to ride with the wedding party, as they were supposed to. They got into a second limo.

That was another sign. An unusual change in behavior. At this point I might have talked to someone about my concerns.

The caravan started down Lido Boulevard, a very long, straight road which led to the posh reception hall, "The Sands at Lido." But shortly after the caravan began it had to be halted. The bride's father, perhaps because of the stress of the event, felt sick and had to throw up. The procession stopped, the father took the couple of minutes he needed, and the procession started up again. That was another sign. The final one.

It was a short ride to the reception hall, and presently the lead limo, carrying the wedding party, turned slowly in toward the driveway leading to the hall. All of a sudden, from out of nowhere, a dragster rocketed around a curve. He couldn't see the limo and the limo driver couldn't see him. Crash. The dragster smashed into the limo at a speed in excess of 100 miles an hour, virtually cutting the limo in half.

The groom was killed instantly, as was his brother, the best man. The bride lingered between life and death in a hospital for two days before she died. (Later her nurse was to report that at one point she had become conscious and said she saw the groom. She had, but he had already crossed over and was waiting for her to join him.) The only person in the car who lived was the other maid of honor, and the dragster himself. (Who says life is fair?) The flower girls lived. They had, remember, switched limos.

In a terrible footnote, the father who stopped the caravan because he was sick blamed himself. If only, he said, he didn't stop. If only. If only. But I try to remind people that sometimes we can't stop these things from occurring, and that we are all human and do the best we can. And who is to know, I would tell that grieving father, how many times his psychic energies saved his loved ones over the years? Like I said before, sometimes we know of our psychic successes—and sometimes we don't.

Looking back, I try to be brutally honest with myself. I don't know if I would have been able to put all these signs together, nor do I know, if I had tried to stop the trip to the reception hall, whether I would have been taken seriously or looked on as a kook. Who knows? But I will always regret one thing for sure: knowing that I had seen this accident seven months earlier when Carmen came in for a reading and not following through on it.

MAKING CONTACT

There's a simple way to get signs from the dead. Take some object left by the person who has passed, such as keys, an article of clothing, a photo, and put it under your pillow at night. Ask that person to send you a sign, and repeat the request every night for a week or so or more. The request can be couched like:

"Hey, Dad, I'd love to hear from you. Please give me a sign that you're around."

"I miss you, Mom. Can you come for a quick visit?"

You can say whatever you want. You don't have to spell it out. Perhaps you have a favorite term that you used before the person passed:

"Hey, cat, where you be?"

"Man, I'm missing you like you wouldn't believe."

"I need your arms, my honey, and I need them soon. Please come back."

Then wait, and be alert, ready for signs. After a while you'll start receiving them, and as you get more and more psychically attuned you'll be able to do this quickly. Don't forget when someone loves you and shows it the feeling is both beautiful and beneficial. Nothing in life—or death!—is more profound.

DÉJÀ VU

- The dead like to leave signs to tell us they're still around and that they love us. Sometimes these signs contain special messages, but mostly they're just loving communications.
- Common signs include smells, sounds, and sudden changes in temperature, but really, the possibilities are endless.
- Signs are usually very simple; nevertheless they can be subtle and hard to spot. Developing your psychic ability—staying open and in tune to the possibility of signs—will help you both to receive and understand these communications.
- You can bring on signs from the dead just by asking for them in your special way.

SIX

Unleashing Your Own Psychic Ability

DEVELOPING A PSYCHIC MIND-SET

One night in the early eighties, when I was a sophomore in college and had just completed one of my first psychic parties in Queens, I was approached by a young woman named Mary.

"You know, Jeffrey," she said, "you might want to meet the Kraus sisters."

"The Kraus sisters?" I asked. "Who are they?"

"Two elderly sisters who live in Jamaica Estates," she said, describing a posh part of the borough.

"So, why should I want to meet them?"

"They're both psychics. Have been for years."

I was thrilled. People with psychic ability were hardly welcome at that time, so the prospect of meeting two other psychics was very appealing to me. Birds of a feather and all that.

"By the way, you said they were elderly. I'm curious. Just how old are these sisters?"

"Helen is in her early seventies," Mary said. "I guess Carol is in her early eighties."

Mary gave me their number and I called the next morning.

"Oh," said one of the sisters. I think it was Carol. "We'd love to have you come over."

"Great."

"Could you make it for lunch today?"

"Yes," I said. "As a matter of fact, I could." That was unusual in itself. Normally I would have been too busy to accept such a last-minute invitation. But apparently not with all that psychic energy flying around!

Promptly at twelve, the time we had arranged, I drove out to a majestic Tudor house in Ozone Park. It was obvious that I wasn't in the same fiscal league as the Kraus sisters—they were in the majors and I was in the minors.

When I rang the bell, the door opened immediately and I was greeted by two small women, each with light eyes and light hair. They seemed ageless, their eyes too alive to betray any trace of the years that had passed. We introduced ourselves and I followed the sisters into the house. They led me through the living and dining room and into the kitchen, a pure fifties setup, with a linoleum floor, cast-iron sink, knotty pine cabinets, and an ancient refrigerator.

"Hungry?" Carol asked.

"Sure." I was always hungry.

They sat me down and, as we engaged in small talk, Helen started putting lunch on the table. I did a double take (or maybe it was quadruple) as they set out macaroni salad, German potato salad, thick-sliced butcher baloney, bratwurst, and a loaf of crisp seeded rye from the bakery.

"These are all my favorites," I exclaimed "How did you know?"

"We're psychic too, remember," Helen said with a little smile. If I didn't know it before I arrived, I knew it now.

Take a second look at ordinary things, particularly if they seem "coincidental." They may not be so ordinary after all.

—The Kraus Sisters

I became close friends with the Kraus sisters, who I quickly came to think of as "The Aunts." Over the next four years while I helped them with chores and errands, they taught me techniques that were to greatly improve my psychic abilities. I'll always be grateful to these lovely women. They gave me such courage and confidence, such pride in my psychic abilities, that I knew that I had to develop them to the best of my abilities. It became my duty, my responsibility—and my calling.

The Aunts told me that the best thing I could do to sharpen my psychic ability would be to constantly test my psychic mindset. As Helen, the younger of the sisters, put it to me: "You have to approach the world with your psychic side active, always trying to determine whether something is psychic or not. If you're just walking along the street, for example, and you see a flash out of the side of your eye, take the time to consider what you've seen. If you have a dream, take the time to ask yourself if it contains a psychic message. If you see a glow around someone, or if the phone rings in the middle of the night . . . try to understand these occurrences and be ready to interpret them as energy coming through to you. Don't just dismiss something as coincidence."

"Of course there are roadblocks to developing the psychic mind-set," Carol continued. "For one thing, it's a sort of alien world, unexplored. The psychic mind-set asks you to look at the world in a completely different way, and that's not always easy. No longer can you take things at face value. No longer can you accept what appears to be. You have to look deeper. Make the connections. Of course you have to be intuitive, but it's more than that. You have to learn how to train your intuition, to understand it and interpret it. And that's not easy.

"What's more," she went on, "setting aside your reservations can be even more difficult. Everybody has doubts. That's only natural. We live in a world that values the here and now, a world that insists that *seeing is believing.* Well, I'd like to tell you otherwise: *Believing is seeing.* Understand that. Know it. Put it into practice. Sure, you're bound to get discouraged—you'll have difficulty reading dreams, for example, or a person's aura may be giving off mixed signals that are difficult to understand. You may even want to give up. But persevere. Trust in your judgment and your instinct and know that you can overcome any roadblock in your way.

"And every day when you wake up, remind yourself that you have a psychic side. Use it. Look for the aura. Listen to your intuitive side. Keep at it day and night and never ever give up."

It's important to be open to psychic events. Be aware of the myriad ways that psychic phenomena can come to you, and be ready to accept it as such.

I had a client named Sam who really wanted to develop his psychic side. He started out great, really working hard at it. But one day a few months after I had given him some advice on how to read auras, he came into my office disconsolate. Indeed, it was a gray aura that I saw around his head, and for a moment I thought he might be sick. He wasn't, though. Just discouraged.

"I can't seem to get my psychic side in gear," he told me. "I thought I was starting to look at things in a different way, but now the world just seems the same to me."

"So what do you do every day to get it going?"

He looked at me, puzzled.

"What do you mean *every day?*"

That was the problem. He was only doing it "every now and then."

"Well," I said, "if you were trying to learn a new language, how often do you think you would have to study."

"Every day," was his reply.

"And if you were studying the piano. How often would you practice?"

"Every day," he said.

"And if you were training for the Olympics . . ."

"Okay! Okay! I get it, Jeffrey!" he said, a little annoyed. "I have to practice developing my psychic ability every day. Point taken."

Use your psychic side every day. And never give up.

Psychometry

"Come into our parlor, "Carol said. "We want to show you something."

They sat me down in the living room and then Carol took a framed photo off a piano and handed it to me. I had noticed the photo when I passed through the living room on the way to the kitchen. Now I took a good hard look. The man in the photo was balding. He had a large handlebar moustache and his clothing looked like it might be from the early nineteen hundreds.

"Who is that?" Helen asked. "Tell us about him."

I was about to say, "I don't know," when suddenly I did.

"He's your brother," I said.

"What else?" Carol asked.

"He was a fireman. He's dead. He also had trouble walking and . . ." I hesitated.

"And what?" Helen asked.

"He had a little trouble with the bottle."

"More than a little," Carol said, laughing.

I was stunned.

"I don't understand," I said. "How do I know all this?"

"It's Charlie's energy," Helen said. "The photo, even the frame, is suffused with information about him and it's flowing from him into you."

"And since you're so psychically open," Carol added, "you are able to understand it."

Abruptly, a name occurred to me:

"Who's Peter Hurkos," I asked.

The Aunts looked at each other and smiled.

"He's a famous crime psychometrist. He helped solve a lot of murders. You're too young to remember, but he worked with the cops on the famous Boston Strangler case in Boston in the early sixties."

"Why is his name coming to me?"

They looked at each other again, a little puzzled.

"We don't know for sure," Helen said, "maybe just because psychometry is what we're talking about and you're picking up specific energy about that."

Psychometry, The Aunts explained, is the ability to read the history of certain objects. Personal objects are best, such as photographs, keys, watches, rings, etc. They seem to give off the most divine facts. Every person, spirit, and object in this world and the next contains psychic energy. That understanding is fundamental to psychometry and to the psychic world.

Well, from that time on The Aunts would give me psychometric tests. Later I learned to use the technique in my practice. I remember the first time, it was about two years after I first met The Aunts. I was called by the proprietor of a large shoe store in Queens who wanted to know who was taking money out of the cash register. One Sunday, when the store was closed I went over to the cash register and laid my hands on it. Immediately I got an image of a cleaning lady. And sure enough she turned out to be the culprit.

Every person, spirit, and object in this world and the next contains psychic energy. That understanding is fundamental to psychometry and to the psychic world.

Another time I had a distraught woman named Celia Mooney come for help to find her young daughter Missy, who she said her estranged husband Marty had abducted.

"He could be anywhere," Celia said, "because he's a toolmaker and goes where the work is."

"Do you have a picture of Missy?" I asked.

"I have a lot of them," Celia said. She went through her wallet which was fat with photos of the little girl. She handed me a small color photo.

"This is the latest," she said. "We took it at one of the photo machines in the mall. She's five."

I took the picture in my hand and bore in on it. Missy was smiling. She had brown hair, brown eyes, and her hair was cut in bangs. And she wasn't self-conscious because she was smiling broadly, this despite missing teeth which made her mouth look like a half-eaten slice of watermelon.

As I stared, I started to get images. I saw a very narrow, sunny street lined with small houses and palm trees, and in the middle of the block a white stucco house with an orange tile roof and a concrete path going through a browning lawn to the sidewalk. On the sidewalk was a little girl riding a battered bike.

The picture was clear, but this was a tough one. What city? What town? What street? I didn't have a clue. Then another image, this time of green water lining the shore of a large body of water. An ocean? But why green water? Why not blue?

I was frustrated. I knew I had seen green water before, but where? Then it hit me. Miami!

The images dissolved as I handed back the picture to Celia.

"How is she?" Celia asked.

"She's fine," I said. "She'd like to see you."

Celia nodded, swallowed. I knew she was fighting tears. She drifted away for a moment, then refocused.

"Where is she."

"I think she's somewhere in Miami," I replied. "Somewhere near the beach. The water is clear, and very green."

"Like I said, Marty is a toolmaker. Maybe we can track him down in Miami."

"I'd bet on it," I replied.

Two days later Celia called me, very excited.

"I contacted the authorities in Miami. They found him. We found her!" she said excitedly. "In Miami, just as you had said!"

Case closed.

Psychometry is an excellent tool for harvesting psychic information. For simplification, you could think of it as a device to turn an ordinary object—such as a ring or picture or key—into a book that you can read psychically. That is, you can use the object to ex-

---

The first time I used psychometry to help the police I got a very frosty reception from a grizzly cop who did nothing to hide his cynicism.

"Here's a clue," he said, handing me an envelope.

"No it isn't," I fired back. "It's your wife's shopping list. And by the way, she forgot the eggs."

---

tract energies that will then flow into you. You can read and translate that energy into usable information.

Like other psychic skills, psychometry takes time and effort to develop. You can work at it yourself by reading other people's objects and "playing back" the energy and information. Hold an inanimate object in your hand. Close your eyes and try to focus on the object. Be attuned to the energies coming from the item—they'll be subtle—and then interpret those energies into information. At first it will feel like you're just guessing. That's fine. Many of our "guesses" actually come from intuition and aren't guesses at all. But as you progress you'll start to know the difference between the information that you produce by guessing, and the information that you can glean from psychic energy.

Like all psychic skills, practice makes perfect—or should I say practice makes psychic. So, to get yourself going, I suggest you set yourself a schedule of psychometry exercises fifteen minutes a day, three times a week. But it needn't be all work and no play.

Psychometry parties can be a lot of fun. The Aunts and I used to have them all the time.

- Gather a group of people together and ask each to deposit an object in a container, such as a paper bag or a cookie jar.
- The object should be something personal—a key, say, or a ring.
- It's important that the owners of each object are kept secret; so make sure that these "deposits" are made furtively.
- Mix up the objects, then one by one distribute them to the crowd. Obviously, if anyone gets his own possession he should return it for another.
- Ask everyone to be silent for a few minutes, then instruct them to hold their items in their hands—not too tightly—and focus.
- Many people will "try" to come up with a meaning for their object, but that defeats the purpose. Trying imposes your will on someone else's possession, and that may block the psychic energy coming through. So instruct your guests to take a breath and let the information come naturally.
- One by one, go through the room. Ask each person to give details about the owner of the object they have in their hands. Some people will clown around, of course. There's at least one in every group, I guarantee it! Some will be blocked and not able to come up with anything, but you'll be surprised by the number of people who are accurate or close to describing the owner of the object.
- You can repeat the game as many times as you like.

Psychometry is really quite fascinating. I remember being at one of these gatherings where one of the participants, a middle-aged man, was able to extract a story from a ring which related to the original owner, the great grandfather of the man who was at the party. The story involved the great grandfather coming over on a sailing ship at the turn of the century. The great grandfather was a boy at the time, and his mother had given him the ring for luck. Well, the Atlantic crossing was an ordeal for the child, who was both frightened and excited by the thought of his new life in a new country. The little boy constantly touched and turned the ring during his trip because it reminded him of the loved ones he had left behind. That energy was still perceptible some sixty years later. It brought some of the people to tears.

Meditation

Meditation is a great tool for the budding psychic, particularly when it comes to connecting with the dead. Meditation encourages you to become very calm. And only when you're very calm and not absorbed by the pressures and concerns of your earthly life can you really reach the dead. Joanie and The Aunts have helped me in this regard, and I'd like to pass along their meditation methods to you.

First, pick a spot that you find comfortable. Some people like the great outdoors, weather permitting. Some go to beaches and some just lie on the deck and take in the rays. I have a couple of clients from the Bronx who say they go up to a place they call "Tar Beach"—the tarpaper roof of their apartment building. They go up there with a blanket, a little half tent, and pitcher of lemonade. It really helps them to get calm. Most people prefer indoors, though. I guess they like the privacy. "I just go into a guest bedroom," says one client, "and that's fine, particularly since I get up early. It's as quiet as the house is going to be all day."

Soothing sounds can also be helpful—soft music or the sounds of nature. A flickering flame tends to be relaxing, so you may also want to set a single lit white candle nearby. A class of water nearby also helps. Just imagine all the chaos and stress being drawn into the water.

Most people prefer to meditate in the morning. "I'm fresh," says one client, reflecting the view of many other people. "At night I'm tired and my concentration tends to wander."

Sit up or lie down, whatever you find most comfortable; but do pay attention to your breathing. Concentrate on breathing through your belly. Take deep breaths through your nose and focus on getting your belly involved. Then let out the air slowly. Again, make sure you are really involved in the process, body and mind, heart and soul. Be aware. Breathing in this manner results in taking in and letting out larger amounts of breath, a process that relaxes us both physiologically and psychologically.

In the end, though, there are no strict rules in meditating. Whatever works to turn you limp is fine. That said, I believe it's important to journal your meditation as you experience it. Journaling tends to reinforce the experience as it's taking place—making it more real—and will also reinforce the meditation *after* the experience. This may seem contradictory, I know. You're trying to relax, but also record what you're experiencing at the same time,

---

Moments from a Journal "Resting in bed, candle lit . . . liked looking at its flame . . . very relaxed . . . feel like I'm sagging inside . . . very, very relaxed, like melting wax . . . ready to climb. The stairs look like always . . . wide, covered with carpet . . . I enter the room . . . beautiful, but empty . . . lime green like always . . . and soft yellow glow . . . nothing . . . across the room are the other stairs . . . such a beautiful room . . . walk across carpeted floor like other times, start to climb carpeted stairs ever so slowly up and up . . . have a feeling something is going to happen this time . . . last time and all times it was empty . . . Almost hear the doorway . . . shadow crosses the doorway . . . there is something in the room . . . up I climb . . . lime green room, yellow floor, beautiful . . . and there is someone sitting in a chair with his back to me. Oh, I hope it's Daddy! Daddy! Daddy! Oh my God, it is. It's Daddy. Daddy, how are you? How are you. Oh. . . . Daddy stands and smiles. Daddy is fine. I start to cry, cry hard. . . . Daddy is gone. But I know he'll be back, I just know it. I know I will! I've talked to Daddy . . ."

---

which is intrinsically distracting. It may seem unnatural, but trust me. It works.

Once you are all nicely settled in a quiet place with your body in a comfortable position, your cleansing glass of water nearby, breathing deeply, the flame flickering a little hypnotically, pray to God to take you to a peaceful place. You don't need to have a formal religion to do this, just pray to a God of your choosing. The point is to place yourself in the loving arms of someone else, a higher power whom you trust and love.

The next step is to visualize. Close your eyes and imagine a peaceful scene. It may be the end of a day, a setting sun, or a green tropical isle set in azure water. One of my clients disappears into the two brown lakes of his grandson's beautiful brown eyes. "I used to have white-coat hypertension, but not since I started visualizing my grandson's eyes," he says.

Relax like this for fifteen minutes or so, then start forming a picture in your mind of a room. A beautiful room, perhaps 10 by 10 feet, with blue walls and a ceiling and a lovely blue carpet. Tell yourself this is the most beautiful room you have ever seen.

Slowly enter the room and look around. It is empty, but breathtakingly beautiful. Then, notice something on one of the walls: a set of steps leading up. These steps are gently beckoning you to climb, but you know you need something else. You know you are going to a place where you need something that can help you perceive another level of consciousness. You need, in a word, a chakra, a third eye in Buddhist terms, the eye that can observe another consciousness. Now, you sense that third eye in you, in the middle of your forehead. This third eye will see things that your human eyes cannot. It will look down the hallway of eternal consciousness.

Start climbing, very slowly, relaxed, looking, looking . . . until you enter another room, and this one, the same size and color as the one below, is breathtakingly beautiful, impeccable, perfect in every way.

Know that it is here that you will meet the dead. And know that it will be good. But understand that it might not be today. Understand that this will take time.

Then, slowly, deliberately, leave the room. Go back downstairs where gently, slowly, you will terminate your meditation.

The next day, or whenever you can, repeat the meditation. It might be difficult because nothing happened on the first day. But look on this as a development, a process that needs to take its own time rather than an event that occurs quickly, all at once. Indeed, look forward to the future for when something does happen. It may take a week, it may take a month or even a year. But rest assured. You will meet with those who have passed.

Visualization

I think of visualization as a close cousin to psychometry, but with a larger scope. Visualization involves conjuring pictures in the mind (hence the relationship to psychometry), but these pictures can be called from the future, not just the past. You might say that visualization not only receives visions, but creates them too.

Visualization is very valuable in helping people achieve their goals. I had one young client who wanted to work for an advertising agency. I told him to imagine himself in the position and to do this every day. He did, and after awhile images formed and became increasingly detailed.

"I imagine myself in my own new office," he told me a few months after we first met. "The room is nicely decorated—beige walls with three landscapes hanging on them—and there is a polished wood desk with a black phone. I am constantly at the desk and on the phone. I'm very busy."

"Still want the job?" I said with a smile.

"Absolutely."

My client continued to visualize everyday, until some three months later he decided he was ready to search for his ideal job. It didn't take long before he landed an interview, and it didn't take long after that to land a position. His new office? True to form: beige walls with three landscapes hanging on them, a polished wood desk, and a black phone. And he is very, very, busy.

Surely there is a grandeur in knowing that in the realm of thought, at least, you are without a chain; that you have the right to explore all heights and depth; that there are no walls nor fences, nor prohibited places, nor sacred corners in the vast expanse of thought.

—Robert Green Ingersoll

So, how to visualize? Start with understanding that visualization is a process of feeling, then reading, the vibrations of psychic energy. Put yourself in the correct mind-set. Relax. Feel. Be positive. Believe in the flow of energy and your place in it. Find a place that you can regard as sacred during your visualization time. It could be a study, a bath, a bedroom. Any place that is calm and quiet. Any place that you can use without interruption. Ask yourself what process of visualization would suit you. Would you like candles, aromatherapy, or music? Would you like the cover of darkness, or would an encouraging brightness suit you better? Consider the setting and the process that would work best for you, then do what you can to make it happen. I tell people to use bubbles, honey flowers, or rose petals to set a conducive atmosphere. Water is very good because it can help to channel away negative energies. I also suggest using prayer to get started. It doesn't matter what your religion is, or even if you have one. Use what's familiar and real to you.

Close your eyes. Relax your mind. Picture the great release you are about to experience. Picture the source of your pain receding. Picture the gradual draining away of negativity and loss. You must cleanse the solar plexus to realize the vibration.

Keep it pure. Sit up straight. Remember to breathe. Take a few cleansing breaths. Relax your shoulders. Feel the release of psychical and emotional pain. Imagine worry falling away. Empty your mind of thoughts, then invite the return of psychic energy.

If you want to visualize your soul mate, for example, take deep breaths and invite that person into your life. Don't try too hard for specifics at first. Just tell the universe that you want to find your soul mate, that you're ready. Leave it open at first. Don't expect. Just ask. Stay calm. Imagine. Breathe. Relax. Breathe. Soon a picture of that ideal person will come into your mind. Be ready to accept the spiritual qualities your soul mate person will have. Think about spirituality before considering physicality. Once you have these aspects in mind, a picture will start to form. Give it time. Give it room. Accept. Be prepared to be surprised.

This process should be at least thirty-five minutes. When you're finished, take a moment to wash your hands. Cleanse your outer shell and release your thoughts. Washing your hands provides a simple release from the world of visualization and a return to the physical world. It signals the end of the session.

Candles can be very conducive to visualization. Use white, orange, or blue. Don't use red—it's too passionate and will interfere with the process.

Anyone practicing the psychic arts can expect to be challenged by others. About a year ago, for example, I was conducting a seminar on psychic skills in New York City when a woman stood up and said, "Visualization just sounds like normal yearnings to get something. I don't see anything psychic about it." I pointed out an important distinction: "Practicing visualization involves an orchestrated, sustained effort. When you visualize, you are deliberately focusing on specifics. That's a far cry from random yearnings or hunches."

Once you've made your first connection you will almost always connect. And the more you do it, the faster those connections will be. At this point in my career—after years of contacting dead people quickly in client sessions and on radio and TV—I get to that upper room, "blue zone," almost instantly. Also, after a while you won't have to set up a special place to connect. You'll be able to connect with the dead while in the office, in your car (watch the road, though!) and just about any place. And psychically, you will have developed a wonderful skill that takes you to places that make Disney World look like a walk around the block!

Stay Calm

Anyone seeking to improve their psychic abilities must understand the importance of staying calm. When you stay calm, you can do everything better. You can hear that little voice, see the gradations in an aura, focus on what you have dreamed, and do a better job of analyzing your behavior. Staying calm means setting aside your emotions and self-interest. Essentially, it means getting yourself out of the way so that you can pick up on the multitude of energies around you. We all know what it's like when we obsess on the details—we can't see the bigger picture around us. Well, the psychic world *is* that bigger picture. So relax. Take a deep breath and put your cares and concerns to one side and *don't* let this be about you.

Learn All You Can

In a way, exercising your psychic skills is a process of desensitizing, getting used to the terminology, engaging in psychic activities, and just plain learning.

Reading books by psychics will really help you in the process. Sure, there are some "psychics" out there who are off the wall, but most are reliable, and reading what they've written will not only help keep you in a psychic frame of mind, but will give you some very practical information. Nobody knows everything, of course, not even me! (As I've said before, I'm psychic, not omniscient.) That's why it's important to read widely and well. I've really developed as a psychic by reading people like James van Praagh, John Edward, Suzane Northrop, and George Anderson. They've helped me shore up my beliefs. Also, because being psychic is a spiritual foray, I've also read a number of spiritual writers, my favorite being Neale Donald Walsch, author of, among other titles,

Conversations with God. And of course because being psychic is associated with the dead, I for one have found the work of Raymond Moody, M.D., invaluable.

Challenge Yourself

One way to test your psychic abilities is to write down a series of questions for yourself when you get up in the morning, then see if you can answer them. Here are some to get you started, but of course you can also make up your own.

- What celebrities or luminaries are gong to cross over in the next two months?
- What is the favorite food of________(pick a person)?
- What country is going to be hit by a natural disaster over the next month?
- Who in your family is going to change jobs in the next year?
- What scandal, if any, is going to hit America in the next six months?
- What romantic relationship that you know to be solid is going to break up over the next year?
- What celebrity is going to have a major tragedy in his or her life over the next six months?
- What is going to be the most popular TV show next year?
- Who in your family is going to have surgery next year?
- Who in your family is going to meet a long-lost friend?

You can consider each of these questions worth 10 points. If you get 8 out of 10, you have a score of 80, which is right up there as a professional psychic. A few years ago a number of psychics, including George Anderson and John Edward, were tested at the

University of Arizona and they scored around 85 percent correct on questions answered by them. (A group of students at the school were asked the same questions and scored 36 percent.)

But don't feel dismayed if you score poorly. You're just starting out. Your scores will get higher as you develop psychically. Incidentally, most of the questions I've given require that some significant time pass. If you're impatient, and would like virtually instant feedback, here are some other questions.

- What color shirt is (such and such a person) going to wear today?
- What person on the job owns a cat?
- What person on the job owns a dog?
- What color is the car of________(pick a person)?
- What is the hobby of________(pick a person)?
- What is your best friend's favorite color?
- What is your best friend's least favorite color?
- What is your boss's favorite TV show?

If you don't score well on these question, as I mentioned earlier, don't worry. You'll do better as you develop—you're just beginning.

When answering these questions, you should try to focus on getting psychic answers, not logical ones, if indeed logic even applies. For example if you pose a question to yourself on the color of shirt a co-worker is going to wear, just think about it. Lay your energy out there, but don't try to work it through logically. Pose it and leave it, and let the answer come naturally. In doing this, your action attracts the energy of the other person, the shirt wearer or whoever, and then you can read it. You have to suspend thinking.

When you evaluate your insights as a psychic, be careful not to be too quick to count yourself as being wrong. Sometimes it takes a little detective work to determine if you're really wrong—or right.

For example once on *The Maury Show,* as I described in the Preface, a woman named Christine had lost two children in a fire and I told her that she had had another child. At first she denied it, but then she remembered that she had also had a miscarriage, which meant that in this instance I was correct.

Many times I would mention a name to a client, say, Barbara, and they would say something like: "I don't have any one in my family by that name." Then they'd think about it some more and say something like: "Unless you mean my Aunt Barbara."

That's exactly who I meant.

I had a client who told his mother that he thought an aunt had been married once, but she said had been married twice. My client and his mother had a discussion, and it was decided that his aunt had been married twice technically, but once religiously, because she had lived her life as a Catholic and had been buried as one. Hence, in the eyes of the Catholic Church she had only been married once.

DÉJÀ VU

- Developing a psychic mind-set is critical to honing your psychic abilities. You have to approach the world with your psychic side active, always trying to determine whether something is psychic or not. Don't accept coincidences. And never assume.
- Psychometry is the practice of reading the history of inanimate objects. Personal objects give off the most "divine facts," and can be used to garner all sorts of psychic information.
- Meditation is a great tool for the budding psychic because it encourages you to become very calm. And you can't tap into your psychic abilities in an agitated state.
- Visualization is key to becoming psychic. The practice of visualization requires an orchestrated, sustained effort in which the practitioner deliberately focuses on specifics and on bringing them into being.
- Practice your psychic abilities daily. Test yourself. Read books by psychics and books on psychic topics. Above all, be open.

SEVEN

What to Do If You're Afraid of the Dead

WE ALL HAVE FEARS

"Have you ever heard the term *scared to death?*"

I was talking to The Aunts.

"A few days ago," I explained, "I had an experience that turned that cliché into my own private reality. I awakened at one in the morning to a room that was bright as day. I lifted my head and looked down toward the end of the bed. I froze. Standing there, looking at me with the blackest, scariest eyes I have ever seen, was this huge Indian, and next to him, a horse. I wanted to turn away, but I forced myself to keep looking. The Indian was dressed all in red. He had on a massive headdress that reminded me of a peacock's tail, and was wearing red pants and a jacket. He had no weapons (no bow and arrow, no tomahawk or spear), but he seemed to me to be very important. A chief, perhaps.

"I was stunned. All I could do was stare.

"Then, the Indian spoke to me telepathically.

" '*Don't be afraid,*' he said, '*I am your protector. I will come again.*' "

"He turned and led the horse into nothingness. They both just disappeared. Me too. I got up and spent the next ten minutes in the bathroom!"

The Aunts laughed heartily.

"When I came back to bed I just lay there for awhile thinking about him," I continued. "He reminded me of my great grandmother Mary whom I've seen in many difficult situations over the years. Maybe he would be serving the same role."

"That's exactly what he is," Carol said, "another spirit guide." Helen nodded.

There are no accidents.

Two days later I visited The Aunts again.

"He showed up again yesterday," I said. "I was driving home after work when I turned my car into my block to look for a parking spot. Usually there aren't any spots on my block, but I look anyway. Well, all of a sudden, I saw a flash of light out of the corner of my eye and there it was: a parking space right in front of my house!

"Do you think it could have been the Indian?" I asked.

"I do!" Helen said enthusiastically. "That's just how spirit guides act. They do all kinds of things for the person they guide, from the heroic to the mundane."

I nodded.

"And he helped me today too. Again, I turned into my block looking for a parking space. And again, nothing. So I circled the block and when I returned there was this guy pulling out right in front of my house! To have that happen once is pretty incredible. But twice? Wow.

"Oh . . . and of course I should mention that I think I saw him out of the side of my eye again."

"It was him," Carol said, "no question."

"Why is he showing up? I have a spirit guide in my great grandmother."

Carol looked at me with an uncharacteristically serious face.

"You need two guides Jeffrey. You have a lot of problems."

They both laughed.

"Seriously, Jeffrey," Helen said. "We don't know why some people get one spirit guide, while others get multiple guides or none. But maybe it does have something to do with you."

"What do you mean?"

"You're a valuable commodity in the psychic world—a pro. Somebody may be paying homage to that."

"Ultimately though," Carol added, "we don't know. It's just the way the spiritual universe works."

"So what do I do?"

"Nothing," Carol said, "just appreciate him in the same way you appreciate your great grandmother."

"He also may be around," Helen said, "because you're going to need him for something important that's coming up."

It didn't take long for that "something" to appear. Two weeks later I was riding the subway at about two A.M., going from the wilds of the Bronx to Astoria, which meant changing trains at Ditmars Boulevard. I was used to traveling the subway late at night—I had to catch the train at four in the morning for my high school job at McDonald's—so I wasn't spooked by the deserted station at Ditmars, not until I got a fleeting thought that I was in danger. Grave danger.

I turned. About 60 to 70 yards away I saw walking toward me a group of maybe ten teenagers, most of them wearing colorful basketball jackets and sneakers. What disturbed me most was that three of them were carrying baseball bats. They sure didn't look like a baseball team to me. I knew that they were one of those "wilding" groups that were famous in the eighties and that they were out to hurt someone.

I figured I was in big trouble, and as they got closer I saw something that confirmed it. One of the guys with a bat was holding the fat part in one hand and rhythmically tapping it in the palm of his other hand and smiling—at me. I forced myself to keep looking. The guy who had been tapping the bat had been joined by another guy who was doing the same thing. Some of the other boys were smiling menacingly too.

I thought about running away, but that wouldn't do me any good. I was too slow. I thought about running into the tunnel. Maybe I could hide in the dark? But if they found me I would be totally isolated from any help. I also thought about crossing to the other platform. There were only four sets of tracks between me and the platform. But it was very risky. All I needed to do was touch the third rail and my mother would be identifying a strip of bacon.

I had no weapon. I couldn't fight them alone. I was screwed.

All of a sudden I heard the train coming. Relieved as I was for a second, I quickly realized it would never get into the station fast enough to help me. Still, I thought I'd try. Just as I was about to make a desperate and—no doubt futile run for it—something appeared in my peripheral vision. The Indian! Standing about 10 yards away, sitting astride his horse which was next to a big ad for suntan lotion, there he was: my spirit guide.

I have never been so happy to see anyone in my entire life.

The Indian looked different than he had when he first appeared to me. Very different. He had the same big headdress, but his clothes were not at all the same. He was wearing a buckskin shirt, buckskin pants as short as a bathing suit, and in one hand he was carrying a wicked looking tomahawk. He turned and looked at me: His eyes were even scarier than before and his face was dabbed with war paint. I was looking at a warrior.

Despite his fierceness he spoke to me gently, just two words: "Don't worry."

The gang obviously didn't see him because they kept closing the gap between us. But then one of them said something and, en masse, they all looked across the tracks to the other platform. I followed their gaze to the two transit cops standing at the bottom of the stairs. They must have just come down. They must have arrived just at the same time as my spirit guide! Abruptly, the gang turned and started to run for it. So did the cops. I watched the drama for a few seconds, before I turned to look at my spirit guide. He was gone.

I stood there as the train squealed to a stop. I was rocked. The appearance by my spirit guide had been incongruous—shocking and moving at the same time. He saved me, I know. The cops didn't show up by chance. The chief had arranged it.

"Few people even scratch the surface, much less exhaust the contemplation of their own experience."

—Randolph Bourne

My attitude toward the Indian shows the mix of feelings I have toward the dead. I've been aware of my psychic abilities for many years and yet they still scare me when they appear. No question about it. But I've learned how to handle them better than I did when I was young, when I would pull the covers over my head or just look away. Over the years I've come to desensitize my fear of the dead based on what I know about them. Now, I let the fear subside so that I may continue to deal with them, because I know the dead mean well. I know they appear in order to help me. In other words, I've been able to put them in perspective. There are even times when I look forward to seeing them. It's like meeting with certain friends who are good news people.

GETTING FEAR UNDER CONTROL

A few years ago a middle-aged man who we'll call Roy came into my office. He was a nervous kind of man, full of energy.

"I want to be psychic," he said, "like you. Can you teach me?"

"Sure," I said. "Why not?"

Over a couple of sessions I taught Roy the basics about auras, intuition, and dreams. But when I mentioned how to begin connecting with the dead I sensed a negative reaction. I let it go.

Roy stopped coming for a while, but then one day about a year after we first met he called and made an appointment to see me. He looked good. His blond hair was shiny and abundant, and there were few wrinkles on his very smooth face. Anyone looking at him would have thought he was doing fine.

Anyone except those able to read psychic energies.

I told Roy that I sensed that he was having problems, particularly with his psychic ability. He confirmed this.

"All the stuff you taught me went by the wayside," he said. "I don't use my psychic powers at all."

"Why not?" I asked.

"A couple of months after I saw you I was really working at developing my psychic side. I was getting pretty good at it. I was starting to see and feel more, just know more.

"Then one night," he continued, "I was alone in the house, watching TV and I glanced through the dining room into the kitchen and I saw a figure, a silhouette, standing by the sink.

"He—or she—was motionless and seemed to be looking directly at me. I figured since my wife was away and there wouldn't be anyone coming into my house unannounced that maybe someone had broken in. But if they had, why were they just staring at me?

"Then I realized something. The figure had the shape of a

man . . . squarish shoulders . . . long neck . . . my dead father's form. It was my father. Just as quickly as I realized it the form disappeared. It took me about an hour to calm down. With the help of some Valium I had on hand.

"From that moment on, and despite the fact that I knew it was my father, who I had loved very much, I stopped trying to develop myself psychically. I knew I didn't have the guts to face the dead, no matter who they were and how they appeared."

I nodded.

"But, Roy," I said. "You *can* do it. There are just some techniques you have to employ and some things you have to realize. One day you'll deal with the dead quite readily. I can show you. Want to give it a try?"

Roy took quite a while to answer.

"Okay," he said, "I guess I could."

I knew he could. That was really why he had come to see me in the first place. To let me help him try once again. And within a few months he not only got his psychic side up and running, but he got to see and converse with his father.

Take a Good Look

There are a number of things you can do to conquer your fear of the dead. Start by looking down the corridor of your life and realizing just how good the dead have been to you. This will go a long way to helping you modify any negative image you have of them.

- Get comfortable. Take a few deep breaths and let yourself relax.
- Now reflect. Look back at your life and see if you can re-

member any occasions when the dead appeared. Try to recall situations where they might have helped you.

- Remember, the dead appear in various ways: human form, dreams, flashes, streaks of light, mists, orbs, shadows, something out of the side of your eye, and just a generalized feeling. And, of course, they leave signs such as smells, temperature changes, music, breezes, and "coincidences." Really, the list is endless.
- Ask yourself: Have you ever experienced any indicators from the dead? Can you link them to good things? Like the day you got that promotion—did you see a flash in the sky? Did you see an orb when you met your spouse? When you were feeling down did you see a shadow and then start feeling good? Or, did you swear you saw, say, your dead mother or father standing in a hospital hallway the night a child of yours who was very sick took a turn for the better? These examples just scratch the surface of experience, but you get the idea.

Once you begin to accept that those who have passed have always had a presence in your life—and chances are, a very *positive* presence—you'll be less likely to be afraid. Remember: Acceptance goes a long way to conquering fear.

Look for the connections between good happenings and the dead. Doing good, remember, is why they come back.

One day, not too long ago, a client named Vic Davis told me a classic appearance story. It sort of reminded me of my own perilous experience in the subway, except in Vic's case he didn't see a dead person.

When Vic was very young he got a job as a manager of a floor finishing supply store on Ninety-seventh Street and Second Avenue in Spanish Harlem in New York City. It was Vic's job to open the store at 6 A.M. every day, even in the winter when it was still dark out.

"One very cold February morning, about 5:30," he said, "I was walking down the street toward the store, which was midway down the block, when two guys turned the corner. They started to walk rapidly toward me. My intuition told me that these guys were going to try to rob me, and I figured there was no way to avoid it. I could never get safely inside the store before they got to me. I just hoped they wouldn't hurt me, but I wasn't optimistic. Bad guys in that neighborhood carried guns and knives. Hardly a day went by when you weren't hearing about violence occurring. Well, I was about 5 yards from the door, the two guys no more than 10 yards from me, when I heard the squeal of brakes and out of nowhere came a battered blue van that stopped squarely in front of the store.

"The van doors opened and out comes these three guys who looked like they were big enough to play linemen for the Jets. The two guys who I was sure were going to rob me walked right past me, obviously more than a little pissed at having lost their mark. One of them gave me a withering glance as they went by.

"I breathed a big sigh of relief, then opened up the store and helped the three mountainous guys buy their floor finishing supplies. As they were deciding what to buy for their job, they kept talking about the diner they usually went to, and how strange it was that it was closed that morning. They couldn't figure out why.

"At the time," Vic said, "I thought of it as a lucky break, but I had just started to get into psychic stuff, so I decided to check it out. A few days later I went to the diner and asked the owner why they were closed the other morning.

" 'It was weird,' he said, 'the opening manager overslept.'

" 'Does that happen often?' I asked.

" 'First time in twenty-three years!'

"The owner may not have had any insight into why his manager overslept, but I did. I sensed it was my grandmother on my mother's side who helped me. She was always good to me during her life, and I've had the sense that she would help me if she could. I don't know why. I just do. So I figure maybe she did a number on that manager so those big guys would show up at my store and keep me from harm."

Trust your instincts.

I think Vic analyzed things correctly. He got the same kind of help from the dead that I believe my client, John Barzac, who was late getting to the building across from the World Trade Center on September 11 got when he wasn't able to find his keys.

So, try it yourself. Look back on your life and ask yourself if there have been instances when illogical things happened to benefit you. Like I've said, I don't believe in coincidence and I don't believe in luck. Things like that happen because they're destined to happen—for you and me.

PUTTING IT IN PERSPECTIVE

Another way to lessen fear of the dead is to think of them in the same emotional perspective as you do religious figures. Ordinary spirits are different from religious spirits—souls who are saints—but they do share the common persona of the spirit. So ask yourself: "Why should I be afraid of one and not the other?" Many of us have an assumption that religious figures are good and mean no harm, while ordinary spirits may be potentially harmful. Not so. Both types of spirits have good intentions.

Try to rid yourself of the Hollywood version of the spirit world. It's false—sometimes dangerously so. According to Tinseltown, the dead are often homicidal maniacs who emerge from slime-covered graves to terrorize the living. Nothing could be further from the truth. But fear sells and Hollywood knows it. They make movies that have us sitting on the edge of our seats . . . and lining up at the box office. It's brainwashing and it's been going on for years so it's hard to fight. Nevertheless, we must try. Keep thinking of how good the dead are. Play G-rated movies in your head. Enjoy them and try to understand them. Don't flee in terror.

FEAR OF THE FUTURE

Let's face it. We're all just here for a short time and the dead remind us of that. They have passed and to us, they represent death, the end of life, and the end of our relationship with our loved ones. When we think about death our minds are filled with images of grief-stricken people at funeral parlors and cemeteries and more. The message beams home: It's so sad to die, and we will die. Everyone will.

To live in hearts we leave behind, is not to die.

—Thomas Campbell

But that isn't true. Death is not the end of life, but the beginning of immortal life. I know this absolutely. I've not only talked with the dead on innumerable occasions, I've been to the other side. I got a glimpse, after all, of the door to Heaven when I crossed over via the psychomanteum. I saw many people who had died and were still "alive" on that side, and I was feeling wonderful. If my great grandmother hadn't tapped me on the back and exhorted me to return to earth, I would have gladly kept walking. Ironically, the thing that disturbed me was having to go back.

Remember that Dr. Raymond Moody interviewed hundreds of people who had clinically died and had near-death experiences. In not a single instance—something that's astonishing when you think about it—did any of the people say they were sad on the other side. And in not a single instance did any of them say it was imperative that they return to life. Indeed, they spoke of being happier than they have ever been in their lives, and very, very reluctant to return to earth.

Just how afraid are you?

It's important for anyone trying to get in touch with their psychic side to deal with any fear they may have of the dead, because as you no doubt know, the dead are a major part of the psychic experience. Eventually they will appear.

I don't really have any magical solution to cure people of their fear of the dead. But even if you can't overcome this fear you can learn to live with it. Making the connection with the dead is an enormously moving and gratifying experience. It is, as they say, worth the price of admission.

DÉJÀ VU

- Fear of the dead diminishes the more we contact them, so be on the lookout for signs. Be open to receiving helpful communications from those who have passed.
- Be aware that you may have a spirit guide, someone who has passed but who can still help you with all kinds of matters, from the heroic to the mundane.
- You can help conquer your fear of the dead by looking back over your life and realizing that you may have experienced good things in your life because of the influence of those who have passed—*after* they have passed.
- Very few people will be so afraid of the dead that they can't function psychically. But like anything else psychic you have to work at it. Connecting with the dead *is* worth the work and courage it may take to achieve.

EIGHT

Readings

WHAT TO EXPECT

Count on being nervous. If you're like most people, you're likely to be a little anxious when you consult a psychic. That's okay. It's natural. I mean, a psychic reading is serious business. You may want to get in touch with someone who has crossed. You may want to explore the answer to a business problem that's been dogging you for years, or you may want some advice on a new relationship. People consult psychics for any number of reasons, all of them important. Why wouldn't you be nervous?

Sometimes the truth can be scary, or even painful, but a good psychic will do all that he can to deliver painful truth painlessly. And although a reputable psychic will try to discern just what a client can handle, it's certainly possible to receive information that you don't want. That's tough. But isn't it better to know than not to know? And isn't it better to air a painful secret in a safe and supportive environment? Sure, I've heard stories of some psychics telling people shocking news. And I've even heard stories of psychics who've told clients that they or a loved one was going to die—and when. Now that's unconscionable, unless the client has specifically asked for that information in order to prepare for the death of a loved one, say, or to work through some issues that the client wanted to resolve before the other party passed. But I would do that only when asked, and then only when I'm sure that the client can handle such heavy information. Certainly I've told people that they may have health issues that need to be explored. I believe it's my responsibility. But never would I blurt out information so potentially devastating as to suggest when someone was going to pass. Why would I?

I once heard a story of a woman who was told by a so-called psychic that her husband was going to die . . . and was then asked by this same "psychic" if she wanted to buy life insurance!

Psychics are not the omniscient beings they're often assumed to be. They're not able to see into the darkest reaches of your soul. They're not going to unlock your buried secrets and broadcast them to the world. Yes, my psychic ability does allow me to unearth a lot of personal information. I've uncovered secret sexual issues, adultery, anger, grief, and thievery—pretty heavy stuff that could be harmful to the client if leaked. But I have *never* revealed anything outside my office without a client's permission, and I never will. No legitimate psychic would. The relationship between a psychic and his client is sacred, like the relationship between a doctor and patient. That bond is precious and revered. To break it would be unconscionable.

The bond between a psychic and a client is a sacred trust.

I try to conduct readings in a soothing, calming setting, as do most other reputable psychics. My office has been designed—and blessed—by a feng shui expert with the goal of promoting peace, harmony, and happiness. It's very calming. The walls are painted light blue, there is a miniature water fountain on my desk, and the room is full of plants. Arrayed on shelves behind my chair are various pictures of my family—my wife and two boys—and assorted bric-a-brac that has special meaning to me. On the carpeted floor, in clear view from the client's seat, there's even a small statue of a golden retriever, symbolizing our dog, Cleo.

My waiting room is similarly soothing. The walls are colored peach. The room has a comfortable couch, a carpeted floor, and lamps with soft-glow light bulbs. Here also are water fountains gently gurgling, two of them positioned on end tables with, I'm proud to say, a collection of *current* magazines. You won't find any 1970s' *Reader's Digests* in my office.

Surroundings do matter. If you're not convinced, consider the story I heard from a New York City police officer about a city jail that was painted bile green, as one guard called it. To lift the inmates' spirits, the administration had the cells painted pink. Everyone, including the inmates, loved it. It had a cheering effect . . . for a while. But about ten days after the new paint job the inmates started to grumble about the color, saying it was too loud or the like. As the days went by, the inmates got more vocal—and obscene.

"I never heard such obscenities, even from prison inmates!" said one of the guards.

Eventually the convicts were at the point of setting fire to their mattresses so the administration had painters come in and go over everything with two coats of the original "bile green." It was an awful color, but in the jail it worked. The inmates calmed down almost immediately. Still think surroundings don't matter?

GETTING STARTED

When you go to your session, try as much as possible to leave your expectations at the door. I know it's not easy, but a psychic can only communicate with those who come through from the other side. He can try to call someone, but there are no guarantees as to whom, and certainly no guarantees as to what. The advice you get may not be the advice you expect!

When I first meet clients I try to establish credibility by telling them things about themselves that I couldn't possibly have known. I know that the burden of proof is on me, psychically speaking, and I want to do what I can to inspire the client's confidence. I won't ask you questions, and I caution you to be suspicious of any psychic who does.

Asking questions is one way of fishing for information, which the unscrupulous "psychic" can then use to make "predictions." A good psychic will tell you about yourself. A scamster will let you do the talking. I urge you to doubt the qualifications of any psychic who starts out a session by asking questions. Trust your instincts. If you feel that someone is fishing for material, they probably are. That's when it's time to leave the session.

When you've seen beyond yourself, then you may find peace of mind waiting there.

—George Harrison

Not too long ago a couple named Paul and Anna Maria Fredericks came to see me from New Hyde Park, Long Island. A psychotherapist and trauma specialist had suggested they book a session. When they came through the door I didn't know what their problem was or what they wanted, but I immediately started to see people appear to me from the other side, and immediately I received various other energies that told me what I needed to know.

First, I saw an old man standing in the room behind them. I identified the man as the father of Mr. Fredericks. Then I saw someone else, a young girl.

"You lost a daughter recently, didn't you?"

They gasped, telling me that in 2001 they lost their seventeen-year-old daughter, Lauren, to leukemia. It was Lauren who had appeared.

I told them how Lauren was dressed. The Fredericks had a closed casket, and had buried their daughter in some very unusual clothing: sweat pants, a favorite T-shirt that was signed by all her classmates, and a blanket which she took with her everywhere. I also told them that there were a great number of people at the wake, and that the casket had contained many pictures that were important to Lauren. Additionally, I was able to tell them about a certain picture hanging in Lauren's high school.

Of course, I got into what Lauren was like. She was a very special girl. Tall and pretty, she had an upbeat attitude and a great sense of humor. She was outgoing and creative and had been accepted at the New York Academy of Film. I had no doubt that one day she would have achieved success.

I was able to tell the Fredericks that a dog also appeared to me, and though I couldn't make out its full name I was able to tell them that its name began with the letter *F.* The Fredericks identified it as being a dog the family once owned named Freddie.

It would have been easy for me to probe just a little bit and use the Fredericks's answers to explore their grief—but I would never do that. Plus, I didn't need to. Lauren appeared to me almost immediately, happy to communicate with her parents through me.

Once my credibility was established and the Fredericks were able to put their skepticism aside, they started talking openly to me, telling me how desperate they were to know how Lauren was doing. I learned from the Fredericks that Lauren had endured a lot of pain. When she was fifteen she came down with lymphoma, and this had developed into leukemia. The doctors tried a bone marrow transplant to save her—a very painful procedure that took five weeks—but sadly, the transplant was not successful. Lauren's parents had been devastated by her death. She had been through so much with her illness their only hope was that, somehow, she was doing okay. I was able to tell them that she was. Lauren looked great. She had a lovely calm look on her face, and all her hair had grown back. She was fine.

The Fredericks, especially Paul, had been doubtful about the whole psychic experience. "I was skeptical," he said, "but all this skepticism vanished. I found the experience astonishing." The experience was very helpful to the Fredericks. Dubious at first, I was able to allay their fears about "all that psychic stuff" and prove to them I was on the level. Most importantly, though, I was able to tell them that their beloved daughter was happy and well.

Believing is seeing.

It's important to be comfortable. If you feel uneasy about the person you're consulting, if something is telling you to be skeptical or doubtful about your psychic's ability or intentions, then pay attention. If your instincts tell you to be on guard, then be on guard. Don't give any information away, and do ask for specifics.

Many so-called psychics will throw generalities at you such as "I see love coming into your life," or "Business opportunities are coming your way." Baloney. What does that tell you?

A reputable psychic should be able to give you details, such as "There's a Mary . . . maybe a Marjorie or a Margaret person coming through . . . Someone with a letter *M*" rather than just "I see an older woman figure, maybe your grandmother?" A reputable psychic should be able to furnish you with dates and names. The psychic won't be right all the time—that's just not possible. But you should be able to notice a pattern of accuracy without having the psychic fish for clues.

Don't answer questions. Don't give information away. Expect details. Be discerning. And let the buyer beware.

HOW OFTEN?

There's one challenge that you may have in seeing a psychic—getting an appointment. I know I'm very busy, booked a year in advance. (I've heard that John Edward is booked up even further!) But remember that not every client keeps an appointment, so if you can get yourself on a list to be able to respond to the first cancellation you'll be able to see someone sooner rather than later.

I only see clients a couple of times a year because I don't want to create a situation where they become dependent on me. Many people try to break this rule, and I've had more than one discussion as to why this is usually a bad idea. My goal is to provide clients with information that will help them make better decisions and live better lives. I am a psychic adviser and I consider myself a psychological enabler—but I'm not a parent.

* * *

There's an old joke about two psychiatrists, one old and experienced, one young and just beginning, who each day ride the same elevator to and from their offices. One night the young psychiatrist says to the old psychiatrist:

"At night you look as fresh and together as you do when the day starts. I'm frazzled and bedraggled. How can you listen to patients all day and look so good?"

"Who listens?" the old psychiatrist says.

Stop, look, and listen. You never know what you'll uncover.

Most reputable psychics really do listen. I know I do. And I will say here that some things that come up are quite rough on me emotionally. Sometimes I even want to cry. But I don't. Not in the office, anyway. If I must, I wait 'til I get home. I can't tell you how many times people have come to me and told me about the loss of their loved ones, including many children. You just can't listen to heartache like that without bleeding a little inside. Of course, now I've developed methods for dealing with it, but sad to say, pain comes before the solution.

TO TAPE . . . OR NOT

For a long time I've allowed clients to tape-record their sessions so they can listen again later. I allow the tapes because I find that some people find it difficult to listen carefully during the session, and listening again at a later date allows them to better understand what I'm saying. It also helps to avoid misinterpretations. That said, I'm a little chary about the procedure because I've found that sometimes these recordings can come back to bite me in the rear! I had one session, for example, where I told a young woman named Ada that I was getting highly negative vibes on her boyfriend, and that she really should consider putting him in her rearview mirror.

Well, one day shortly after I was about to leave my office when a heavyset, bearded man with blood in his eye burst into my office.

"What the f____," he said, "why did you tell Ada that I was no good for her? Who the f____ are you to tell her that? I'm going to knock you on your ass."

The best way to handle a charging animal is to stand your ground, so that's what I did here. I told the guy that he very well might knock me on my ass, but if he did he would land in a big hill of trouble for himself. He hesitated, snarling . . . then left the office in a huff.

FINDING A PSYCHIC

Finding an honest, competent psychic is very important. Beware of scamsters. They will, as the saying goes, rob the eyes out of your head and come back for the holes. I had one client, Monica, who explained to her "reader and adviser" that she had had severe disagreements with her mother who had passed. The reader and adviser faked Monica out by making her believe that she had connected with Monica's mother, and that all would be well. But first Monica had to part with forty thousand dollars for various "blessings."

Anyone can be conned, even Einstein's grandson. People consult psychics because they want communication about something that is very important to them. That means they're vulnerable and in the grip of emotion, that their critical faculties aren't working as they should. Even the most cautious of us can be duped when we're overcome with sentiment.

Another client, a brilliant physicist who could have had a meaningful conversation with Stephen Hawking or Einstein, had lost two family members in a car crash. Emotionally he was in a horrendous state and very vulnerable. Well, not to put too fine a point on it, but this brilliant man ended up buying "special candles" from a reader/adviser for the stomach-tightening sum of one hundred thousand dollars!

I loathe these scamsters. Not only do they take advantage of people, but they pollute the image of legitimate psychics. I was never so happy as the time I was able to administer a little payback. I went to a gypsy scamster at the San Gennaro street festival in New York. As she ladled out her hogwash to me I just sat there looking at her. She was trying to butter me up, telling me that I had the look of an athlete and that I was destined to run a big race—and win! When she was finished I spoke to her in a low, pleasant voice telling her that I was, in fact, a psychic and unless she cleared out of the area I would be running her down to the local jail. She was gone within minutes.

If someone tries to drive home a point with fear, you should be very wary. Fear is the con man's stock in trade. Phony psychics like to dazzle their unsuspecting clients with phony curses and damning predictions. If a so-called psychic starts talking in a manner

---

Fear is the main source of superstition, and one of the main sources of cruelty.

—Bertrand Russell

---

designed to make you afraid, if he—or she!—starts talking about black magic and the like, well, you know you are dealing with a con. Sometimes these unscrupulous psychics actually do have ability and are able to hone in on something accurate, but then they may take that accurate information and scare you into coming back frequently, and parting with a great deal of money.

The best way to get involved with a legitimate psychic is to ask around. Have your friends or co-workers consulted a psychic? Did they have a positive experience? Another good way is to contact someone who is prominent on radio or TV, someone who has a magazine column, or has written a book. The reason? Generally, radio and TV stations and publishers vet these people. They surely don't want their good name linked to a charlatan or thief.

Some people, of course, have questioned my qualifications. It's a legitimate inquiry. Degrees aren't awarded in my trade. Sometimes, however, queries or criticisms are off the wall. The biggest nonsense I was ever subjected to was on my WEVD radio show. Someone called up and said:

"How do I know that you're not having fifteen or twenty friends call up and act as if they're strangers?" I told him that if I were that desperate a con man I wouldn't be on radio. I'd be working a pyramid scheme.

SAMPLE READING

Here is a transcript from a reading I recently conducted a few days after Christmas 2002. The names have been changed to protect the privacy of those involved.

I'll call the client "Alice Keller." Alice is forty-one years old, a dark-eyed, dark-haired woman. She's attractive, but a bit overweight. Alice came to see me in my Port Washington, Long Island office a couple of days before she was to fly back to her home in Florida. She had almost completed all educational requirements to get a license for teaching special ed.

Alice is married to "Bob," a computer technician who, in the words of his wife, is "painfully thin."

Bob and Alice have two children, a ten-year-old boy named "Jonathan" and a baby girl named "Lucille" who was twelve months at the time of the reading.

Note how in spots the session seems disjointed. It's because the energies that are coming in—from the living and the dead—arrive when they want to and I have to interpret then and there.

J: Your big problem is your marriage.

A: Why?

J: You treat your husband like he's your child rather than your husband.

A: *(Pause)* I think you're right.

J: It's [your marriage] very much an issue with your identity because you're trying to find out who you are.

A: *(Sigh)*

J: And if you want the marriage to work in the long term you have to do this, find your identity.

A: Okay.

J: He's very involved in his own world and emotionally speaking if you don't have the balance of that you can have problems and you have to watch because with all his family stuff he's not going to change.

A: There's a lot . . .

J: A lot of dysfunctional energy with this.

A: Oh yeah, we (me and Bob) were just talking about it.

J: And it's something you have to pay attention to because you're an enabler by nature. I think the special ed is one big part but I think you're going to go even farther than that because I see a lot of other education.

A: Farther than special ed?

J: Yeah. I think you may end up doing something that's like therapy related. . . . that's related to special-needs kids.

A: Okay.

J: And I think that's going to be part of the premise of what you're dealing with because the problem you have in the marriage is he ignores things. . . . he doesn't deal with things. . . . it's an emotional parallel. . . . it ties in with your Dad and the whole karmic element of the family which is from his side. . . . from the grandmother, grandfather, that you have to pay attention to . . .

A: Okay.

J: Plus there's the energy of another baby.

A: I was thinking I was done. I have my little boy and little girl. . . .

J: There's still the energy of another little girl.

A: Really. Wow.

J: That concerns me only because you don't want to give up who you are. Pay attention to that process. . . .

A: Could it not be a baby? Something . . .

J: No. This is what this represents.

A: Can I ask you questions?

J: Yeah. But you just have to pay attention to all this because this is so important it's taking you so long to get your identity . . . so long to take care of you and it's like you have to do this right now . . .

A: I have to . . .

J: Really grow and get yourself together. Babies are fine. . . . Lucy will give you a good run for your money.

A: I already got a good run for my money!

J: You have to watch for some allergies with them, skin problems and they're showing me something with the ear, so make sure you watch that. . . .

A: Oh my goodness. The ear? My husband has psoriasis and he is worrying about my son getting it. . . .

J: He's going to have a form of it but not on the same level.

A: Wow . . .

J: The reason your husband has psoriasis is because he doesn't deal with any of his emotional stuff. . . .

A: Yeah, they said once that stress can cause it.

J: He puts himself under stress. . . . he's got this whole technical side to him. . . .

A: Oh my God . . .

J: He doesn't deal with anything else. . . . he's very layered.

A: Totally him.

J: It's Mommy not giving him the approval. . . .

A: That's totally him. He's in a job now. . . .

J: I don't think he's going to stay with this job. It's a stepping stone.

A: Really? Because there's all this hope of being able to retire early. . . . and he thinks it's a stepping stone.

J: Something else. You don't want him retiring early. You don't want him home.

A: Wow.

J: You don't want him home because believe me he'll get worse. He needs to feel productive. . . . he's a very structured person.

A: Wow.

J: You don't want him out of that meat-and-potatoes element.

A: Okay.

J: His mother is here now.

A: Whose mother?

J: Your dad's mother.

A: Grandma Ryan? What the heck is she doing here?

J: She wants to let you know that you're important to her. She feels there's a parallel between you and her which means you're very similar. That's why she's coming through.

A: And my mother had a question, wanted me to ask you about Grandma Vitello and her sister Aunt Marie.

J: Oh yeah, they're here. I hear of her as Lucy.

A: My Lucy is named after her.

J: I know. She's very honored about that.

A: Oh my goodness.

J: Yeah, they're actually making me feel that all the good cooks are coming from that side because they were very good in the food area.

A: You know I'm in a lot of turmoil now because when I moved down to Florida my mother . . . our relationship goes back. . . . there's a history to it. . . . I'm very connected to her, very attached. . . . but I've grown. . . .

J: The whole point of the last five years was to get on your feet, get your identity. . . . you never would have done it if you stayed home. . . .

A: Yes . . . yeah . . .

J: It had to be on that level. . . . that's why you're going through this. . . . Now there is a Mar or a Margaret that keeps coming through.

A: Well, Mary is my father's mother. I know there's a Margaret. . . .

J: There's also a John. . . . a Jo name that keeps coming through . . .

A: Oh, there are Josephs. . . . my grandfather's middle name is Joseph. . . . so you're saying that right here now you're seeing . . .

J: And she's honored about the name.

A: Really.

J: Very much so . . .

A: Now Celia is her middle name after Bob's grandmother.

J: Yeah, she's pushy.

A: *(laughter of recognition)*

J: Very, very strong . . . a small woman . . . reminds me of Napoleon . . .

A: Wow . . .

J: She's also very meticulous. Everything has to be done a certain way. . . .

A: Wow . . .

A: Now Bob's mother asked me to ask you if she was doing the right thing. . . .

J: The grandmother that passed feels that she has to follow

her heart, that it has to be done in that way even though people are not going to like what she's doing, this is what she should do.

A: Okay, should I tell you that she's trying to get this house?

J: From who?

A: There's a whole ugly estate thing.

J: There's two brothers involved in this?

A: Yes. There's a David and . . .

J: The grandmother is showing me an older male that is trying to call the shots. . . .

A: That might be David. . . . this is a house we lived in and I remember you told my father that we were going make a move. . . . and boy did we move. . . . to Florida. We're not nuts about Florida but for me therapeutically . . .

J: You have to get away. . . .

A: I'm going to finish, get my degree. . . .

J: You have to do that. It's important. And you have a lot of his artistic ability too.

A: Do I?

J: You know it. But you take something and then you don't move forward with it. You have to pay attention to that.

A: Yeah, I do. I don't know if it's me but I want to go see Joanie [another psychic]. She lives five minutes away from me. Is that fate or what?

J: Yeah.

A: Five minutes away and she said that either me or someone had some kind of ability.

J: Absolutely.

A: And we don't know who it might be. More like me.

J: You were the buffer for your Mom and your father in

their relationship because they had to work their stuff out. . . .

A: I feel very guilty easily.

J: Get over it. Be careful with your relationship with your husband with that because that is a very big issue. That's why it's important right now that you have your identity worked on. . . . this is the thing that's going to get you to where you want to be. This is your next step of being, your next step of growth, your next step. . . . this is going to be the thing that's going to make you happy. . . . because he's not going to change . . . he's very black or white.

A: Okay.

J: You can't enable somebody. He has to be responsible for his actions.

A: Okay.

J: He has to work on the politics of that job. If he works on the politics . . .

A: Oh yeah.

J: He's not good with politics. . . .

A: He's not.

J: No, he takes it as if it's a personal attack on him.

A: Totally. He gets to the point where he thinks what they think is right. . . . it's something I do too. Have to get away from that.

J: I know your grandmother says your mom was not originally thrilled with him, totally not thrilled . . . she thought you married down.

A: Grandma Cathy?

J: No, Grandma Mary. She's saying that they felt like you were settling with this guy.

A: She met him too. People who meet him are turned off. . . .

J: Argumentative.

A: Yes. Argumentative.

J: Well, he's angry. Angry because he's a victim. But you have to be very careful. That's what this is all about. You have to get into not being his mother.

A: Yeah, I'm the mother to everybody.

J: And because of it you're never going to get into your own identity.

A: I can tell you how bad the guilt runs.

J: Well, get over it. You have nothing to feel guilty about. The thing you need to pay attention to is that you have a right to be a person, you have a right to being. . . . the more you pay attention to who you are the better it's going to be. . . .

A: When we got our new car I actually felt guilty, I cried because of people who could not afford a new car.

J: That's not your fault. You need to be less fearful, and the more you are the better it's going to be.

A: I don't have enough confidence in myself. . . .

J: Well, hello, look who we're married to.

A: Yeah.

J: I mean your kids are going to be fine. But watch your daughter, she's definitely going to challenge the authority. Also, your son and your husband have a lot of karma in their relationship and he needs to get a lot more sensitive to the boy and pay attention to the kid.

A: Is he [Jonathan] going to be okay? I've been brought to tears. This poor kid. He's been diagnosed with ADHT.

J: That has nothing to do with his intelligence. You just have to work with it.

A: Yeah . . .

J: Your husband has it on some level too.

A: He's been diagnosed with bipolar also.

J: Yeah, that's what I said. You have to pay attention to this, but my sense of this with your son is that he's going to be okay.

A: Lucy's going to challenge, huh.

J: She has a very strong will.

A: Yes, she does. If she wants something . . .

J: Who is this friend that you lost?

A: Friend that I lost?

J: There's female energy here of a young lady.

A: Friend that I lost?

J: Yeah. May be a teenager . . . also now a male is energy here.

A: As teenagers we lost a friend named Scott. . . . I'm trying to think of a female energy.

J: There's two energies here—two different energies.

A: Right.

J: Comes through . . . like a Mark or a Michael coming through . . .

A: This was my teenage years?

J: Yeah, your teenage years.

A: I don't know. I'm very nervous now, can't think too well.

J: Well, it's very important that the more you do for yourself right now the more it's going to help you deal with life. You're at a crossroads.

A: I can't believe Grandma Ryan came through.

J: Absolutely.

A: We joke about her because she used to come up to me and say "You're my favorite."

J: Even with all the problems that she had she always thought you were the most dynamic of the group.

DÉJÀ VU

- Consulting a professional psychic can be very useful in dealing with a range of issues, some of which may be highly charged. It's natural to feel nervous.
- Sad to say, not all psychics are legitimate. Be wary of those who ask a lot of questions up front—*fishing*—and be especially careful of those who ask you for large sums of money or who try to motivate you with fear.
- Want to consult a psychic? Ask your friends and family. A referral is often the best way to go. You might also check out those you see on the media—on legitimate TV and radio shows—and of course those who have written books.
- Listen to what your psychic says about frequency of visits. It's important not to go too often. (I personally limit client visits to two or three times a year. It's important they don't become too dependent.)
- Be patient. You may have to wait up to a year for an appointment, but chances are you'll find the experience worthwhile.

NINE

Catching Criticism

AVOIDING CRITICISM

I feel well qualified to tell budding psychics how to handle criticism. I've had plenty of it—mostly from myself.

I've always been self-conscious about being psychic. I never wanted to be known as an oddball, so as I was growing up I took great pains to avoid criticism by hiding the things that made me different. I think most kids do. I didn't really become aware of my psychic ability until I was about nine or ten. At first I just thought that "seeing" was something that everyone did. Boy, was I wrong.

One day all my fears came tumbling in on me. I was around eleven or twelve at the time. I had a paper route, one of my first real responsibilities. I would deliver the papers daily and would collect the money from my customers once a week. Typically, after I completed my collections I would drop the money off at the

---

People only see what they are prepared to see.

—Ralph Waldo Emerson

---

newspaper office, and on the way home from there I would walk past an apartment house where a couple of cute blonde girls would be sitting on the stoop. I would stop and talk with them, indulge in a few romantic fantasies, and move on.

One evening, around dusk of a chilly November day (I remember it was getting dark and snow was threatening) I walked by the stoop hoping to see the girls. Too bad for me, they weren't there. I did have company with me, though, a kid named Freddie who had the route next to mine. Well, Freddie and I continued to walk down the block, when after just a few steps I looked across the street to the Lutheran cemetery. The cemetery was normal in every way. It was lined with a spiked fence, crowded with stones and monuments. But on this night I saw movement that made me stop. Freddie stopped too.

"Look Freddie," I said, "a soldier. A Hessian, I think." The soldier, who I recognized from a history course, had a red uniform, a hat, and a musket on his shoulder.

"What soldier?"

"The one in the red uniform, marching back and forth between those two tall monuments."

"I don't see anybody."

"There's someone there."

I pointed out exactly where I saw the soldier. Freddie looked at the cemetery again, then at me.

"What, are you on drugs or something?"

"I see someone."

Abruptly, I realized that I was the only one to see the soldier. Freddie's psychic side was dormant, I was to realize later. Well, I didn't want to make any more of a fuss, so I shut my mouth and we went on our way without further comment.

Once home I allowed myself to worry. I mean, what if Freddie told someone about the soldier? What if people started asking questions? What would I do? What would I say? I'd be laughed out of school. I'd have to leave the neighborhood, change my name . . .

Lucky for me Freddie let it drop. I breathed a sigh of relief at that one.

**To avoid criticism, do nothing,
say nothing, and be nothing.**

—Elbert Hubbard

A little while after that I was hanging out with a classmate named Bruce when I started to get a pain in the center of my chest. At first I thought it was something I ate, but then a picture came into my mind, an image of a heavyset, elderly lady with a fleshy face, large blue eyes, and short gray hair. She was wearing a brown dress and brown shoes. Once this picture became clear in my mind the pain in my chest really started to come on strong. I knew instantly who it was.

"How's your grandma," I asked Bruce.

His brow furrowed.

"My grandma's dead."

"No, the one on your mother's side."

"She's fine."

"Nothing wrong with her?"

"No."

"She's not sick?"

"No, what are you saying?"

"Nothing," I said.

About a week later, Bruce came up to me in a hall at school. Again his brow was furrowed.

"My grandma's in the hospital," he said. "How did you know she was sick?"

"I didn't," I said, a little frightened. "Um . . . I was just making conversation." Which of course, wasn't true.

He kept looking at me—suspiciously—and then walked away.

That incident really scared me. From that moment on, I made sure that I didn't make any psychic observations. To anyone.

My concern about being regarded as a weirdo continued into high school. Belonging is always important to a kid, even more so during adolescence. High school is a time when kids are developing their sense of self big time, where insecurity is as common as Kansas wheat, and where the pace is frenetic, no matter what the school. (I once heard high school described as a combination of "sweat, perfume, and emotion." Boy is that right!)

I used to think anyone doing anything weird was weird. Now I know that it is the people who call others weird that are weird.

—Paul McCartney

I had a strong fear of being "exposed" in high school, and I'm not the only one. Connie Parker, a client and athlete with a heightened sense of her own psychic ability, told me that she was always able to predict how school sports events would turn out, and desperate not to leak the information. "I was petrified," she told me. "If there's one thing worse than being a female jock," she told me, "it's being a female jock psychic!"

Still, that was then and this is now. Thanks to the trailblazing work of people like Shirley MacLaine and John Edward, and thought-provoking movies like *Ghost, Sixth Sense,* and *A Stir of Echoes,* the resistance to things psychic is really being eroded. People are more open now, more willing to believe that there is another side to life—more than meets the eye. In fact, according to a recent poll, a whopping 50 percent of people surveyed said they believe in ESP, 40 percent said they believe in demonic possession, and 33 percent said they believe in ghosts. That's a heck of a lot of believers. And that's terrific!

It's important to feel that you can be yourself in all aspects of life. Why exclude your spiritual capacities and psychic abilities?

Looking back over my own life I can see a strange irony—that by trying to avoid the pain of criticism I've actually encouraged another kind of pain, the kind that comes with secrecy. Secrets can be a breeding ground for unhappiness, so I urge you to consider coming clean about your psychic interests and abilities when you can. You can spend so much time trying to conceal your ability that you forget its beauty and strength. Don't let this happen to you. Psychic ability can give you an opportunity for a more expansive life. If someone isn't evolved enough to accept or understand, well, there's nothing you can do about that. As John Woodward once said, "You can't let praise or criticism get to you. It's a weakness to get caught up in either one."

TIME TO TELL

So, how do you tell someone about your psychic side? I think it depends on who you're telling. A client of mine, a cop named Lou Russo, had honed his psychic ability to the point where he could communicate with the dead. One night over dinner he just flat out told his wife.

"Emily," he began, "I've been learning psychic skills for some time now, and I'm really coming along. In fact, I've been able to talk with my father, my mother, and my brother. I've spoken to some of your relatives too."

"Sure, you have," she humored him. "Now pass me the peas."

"Obviously, Emily was a skeptic," Lou told me, "so I decided that I had to prove myself. That was fun. First I passed on some information that had been passed on to me. I told her that she was going to color her hair, and that she was going to get a promotion. Her response? 'You don't need to commune with the dead to know that I'm eventually going to color my hair. Just look at all the gray! And as for a promotion, well, of course I'm going to get a promotion, Lou. I've been working very hard for a very long time. I'm next in line. You don't need to be psychic to know that.' "

When information about the future didn't do it, Lou decided to turn to the past, telling his wife some things about her childhood that she had never shared. "That did the trick!" Lou told me with a smile. Now she's working on developing *her* psychic side.

If you've honed your psychic skills so that you are able to see things—and maybe even speak to the dead—don't assume that you have to keep it to yourself. You don't!

Telling people on the job can be trickier, though. Not everyone is receptive to the psychic world, and you run the risk of having your co-workers regard you as something of a lunatic, or worse, someone to be afraid of. So go slowly here. Reveal your beliefs and abilities only when you are sure they will be accepted. Happily, your psychic abilities can help you make the correct decision!

I know one person, Jan, an investment counselor, who had honed her belief in the psychic skills very well. Although eager to share her newfound abilities, her spirit guide told her not to share the knowledge with the people at work, especially her boss. She decided to honor that advice and stay silent.

One day at work she was sitting at a table close to where her boss was sitting with some other people. Jan overheard him talking about a TV show that he had happened on called *The Dead Zone,* in which the protagonist is a psychic. It was one of Jan's favorite shows.

"What a lot of baloney," he said to the others at the table, "you have to be slightly moronic to believe in that stuff." Jan was dying to tell her boss that the reason she hadn't told him about her psychic skills was because her spirit guide told her he would be critical. "My boss would have been surprised too," she laughed, "if he knew that my insight in not getting us into a big investment deal, which saved us a ton of money, came from my psychic side."

Fools rush in where psychics fear to tread. Take your time. Reveal your beliefs and abilities only when you are sure they will be accepted.

Another client, Luke, decided to tell his boss about his abilities, with results that were favorable—and highly ironic. Not only did Luke's boss accept his psychic abilities, but she responded by telling him that *she* was psychic as well. As Tracy said: "I always sensed there was something special about you!"

So, how do you know who to tell and who not to tell? You have to know someone very well before divulging something so important as your psychic ability. Don't give up this information casually. Be responsible for what you say. Be appropriate. If someone is critical and closed minded, then chances are they won't be receptive to what you have to say. Look for clues. If someone is always using words like "weird" or "strange," chances are they won't be open to what you have to tell them. Use your judgment. Use your instinct. When in doubt, don't say a word.

THE BEAUTY OF ACCEPTANCE

In my own case, despite life-long concerns about being regarded as strange, I never had any doubt that I would one day meet someone who would be completely receptive to my psychic side. I also developed a profile in my mind of this someone, a profile that was confirmed by The Aunts. She was going to be pretty, blonde, a nurse (something I knew since I was seven years old), the oldest of four kids, live near the water, and come from a family that loved boating. And I thought of her not just as my future wife, but my soul mate, someone linked to me spiritually.

My soul mate came into my life one November night in 1987 when I was on my way to a favorite hangout, a bar named Fin McCool's in Port Washington. Fin McCool's was one of those great New York places where the Mets hung out. That was catnip for me.

Well, one night my friend Peter and I were driving toward the bar when he mentioned that he had met a girl there.

"She has a sister, Jeffrey," he said. "Her name is Dawn."

A thunderbolt.

I felt a surge of energy, a raw excitement that I had never known.

It's her.

"Is she a blonde?" I asked.

Love is the immortal flow of energy that nourishes, extends, and preserves.

—Smiley Blanton

"Yes, as a matter of fact, she is," Peter replied.

"She's pretty too, isn't she."

"Yes. Very pretty, as a matter of fact."

"Peter," I said cautiously, almost afraid to continue. "Is she . . . is she a nurse by any chance?"

"Wow," Peter said, shocked. "You're good. Yes! She is a nurse."

Apparently Dawn was a "step-down nurse," someone who goes into action following surgery. She worked in the heart surgery unit at Long Island Jewish Hospital in New Hyde Park and was very devoted to her profession.

"Why the interest?" Peter asked.

"She's my soul mate."

"Anybody else, Jeffrey, and I'd suggest maybe you meet first. But you I believe."

Peter was well acquainted with my life as a professional psychic. He just nodded. He knew exactly what I was saying.

I couldn't wait to get to McCool's. Thank goodness Peter was driving, otherwise we might have had a traffic ticket, or worse.

Well, we walked into the bar and there she was.

And I knew.

I just knew.

I was introduced to the two girls, and I did my best not to stare at Dawn as I imagined our life together. We stood around making small talk for a while, then Dawn did something that gave me great encouragement. She smiled at me, very warmly. That was all I needed.

In a very natural way, Dawn explained her background, and though she was mostly just repeating information I already knew, all I did was nod.

She *was* the oldest of four kids.

She *did* live near the water.

She and her family *loved* to go boating.

There was more, small details that I hadn't intuited, but basically, everything was as known. And then she asked the inevitable.

"What do you do for a living, Jeffrey?"

I held my breath, knowing that my answer would decide the fate of our relationship right then and there. And I knew which way it would go.

"I'm a psychic."

She didn't miss a beat!

"Oh," she said, "that's interesting. My mother is into that, tarot cards, the whole thing."

"How about your father?"

She paused.

"My father's an electrical engineer," she said. "He wants scientific proof for everything. I think he thinks my mother is a little kooky."

I nodded. I didn't need my psychic side to know that I would likely have trouble with her father.

So we continued to talk and I sensed a warm and caring person. Better still, I had never met anyone who was so direct. When she was finished giving her opinion I just knew that she was holding nothing back.

A short while into our conversation—perhaps a half hour—I took a deep breath and assembled my courage.

"You're my soul mate," I said. "We're going to get married and have three children, two boys and a girl."

That might have sounded arrogant or even crazy to another woman. But not to Dawn.

She just smiled.

Destiny is not a matter of chance, it is a matter of choice. It is not a thing to be waited for, it is a thing to be achieved.

—William Jennings Bryan

Things moved along quickly with Dawn, and it wasn't long before I had to endure that potentially terrifying ordeal, "Meet The Parents." Her father, of course, was problematic. Usually a laid back sort of guy, he gave us a lot of grief at the start. You see, just prior to meeting me, Dawn had ended an engagement with some guy who, by the way, was cheating on her, and when her father heard that she was smitten with a professional psychic he thought that maybe she had gone off the deep end.

I could see his point of view. How would I react? She comes off a broken engagement and falls in love with a psychic—a profession that had quite a different image in those days. Dawn's father actually sent her to a psychologist to see if she was suffering from a mental breakdown. Once the psychologist gave her a clean bill of health, emotionally speaking, Dawn's father had to realize that she was serious about me. That was kind of hard to take. He was used to the straightforward manner of his daughter—she's very direct—but the frankness of a psychic is something else altogether. For some people it's very hard to accept.

I wish I could tell you that I did a reading or some kind of parlor trick and that Dawn's father started shaking my hand and slapping me on the back and telling me how remarkable I am. But he didn't. That's the stuff of TV shows, not real life. I had to give it time. I had to let Dawn's father see that I was on the up-and-up, and that I wasn't some kook out to take advantage of his daughter. You know that old saying, "Time will tell"? Well, in this case it did.

THE CRITIC

You're in for some criticism for your psychic beliefs and ability. I guarantee it. Some people simply do not believe in anything out of the ordinary. If they can't see it, taste, or touch it, they can't believe it. Here are some comments you might expect to hear:

"This is coming from the devil."

"This is the work of a fallen angel."

"You're just in it for the money."

"These are demonic spirits."

"You want to control people. Shame on you."

"You're just a nut job!"

"You must have a microphone hidden somewhere so that you can hear people talking."

"Those are lucky guesses. Nothing psychic about it."

"You must have looked this up on the Internet."

It's amazing how ignorant otherwise intelligent people can be. It can hurt, these comments, but trust me. The more you hear, the easier they are to take. After a while, you'll learn to laugh at them, as I do. Remember. You can only be responsible for your own attitudes and behavior. You can't be responsible for other people—not for what they think, or what they say. So accept that you're going to get some criticism. Learn to shrug your shoulders and move past it. And my last word? If someone criticizes you . . . consider the source!

DÉJÀ VU

- The psychic world has gone mainstream and psychics are accepted as never before. Still, many people are critical of psychics and the psychic experience. Know this going in and you'll find yourself better able to deal with criticism.
- Sharing your psychic ability is a large part of the psychic experience, so don't assume you have to keep it to yourself.
- Be prudent. Reveal your beliefs and abilities only when you are sure they will be accepted. Be especially prudent in the workplace.
- Take care when telling someone at work or in some other situation where it could affect their view of you in a negative way. And use your psychic skills to determine how these people feel about anyone who is psychic.
- You can count on some people being critical, no matter what.
- Try not to be too critical of yourself.

TEN

Cleansing Yourself of Pain and Negativity

PSYCHIC PAIN

The problem was one of those stealthy things that creep up on you. I noticed it one rainy night during the beginning of my junior year. I was trying to get to sleep, but just couldn't. I kept thinking of one particular case, and it was making me sad and depressed. I slept some, but three times I woke up gasping for breath. I was alarmed and thought I might have a sleep apnea or some other nocturnal medical problem. At first I didn't seem able to make the connection between my physical problem and the case that was troubling me. Then, as dawn broke, I started to put it all together. It *was* the case. Of course it was.

I had received the call three days earlier. A woman I'll call

Joanna told me that her nine-year-old boy, her only child, Anthony, had hanged himself after receiving a bad report card. Joanna was devastated. She was living every parent's nightmare, and she wanted desperately for me to contact her son so she could make sure he was okay.

Every fiber of my being resisted. Still, I knew I had to go. This kind of case comes with the territory and I felt a responsibility to this mother and her son. I was very young then, but already I knew I couldn't just pick and choose among my clients, that I couldn't take on cases based solely on what bothered me and what didn't. Don't get me wrong. I'm not John Wayne. I know I'm not invincible. There have been cases that I should have taken on, but didn't. But I'm proud to say that I have never tried to avoid a session just because the pain level was too high.

I accepted Joanna's invitation to visit, and in the morning I drove out to her home in Staten Island. The house was gorgeous. A huge, two-story building with a grand entrance dominated by large white pillars, it was situated on top of a gently sloping hill with a huge greensward as perfect as any golf course. The long driveway was lined with so many small lights it could have been used as an airstrip.

A lot of people would have been impressed. I wasn't. As I drove slowly up the perfect (and perfectly expensive) Belgian-block driveway, I started to get bad feelings coming from the house. Very bad feelings. The choking sensation returned and I felt a tightness in my chest. I tried to gulp down air, but that only made things worse.

I was getting more and more nervous. I parked the car (my old jalopy looked ludicrous next to two sleek Jaguars and a brand-new Mercedes), went up to the front door, and rang the bell. As I stood waiting for the door to open I heard a keening sound that I thought was going to implode my eardrums. It was from a human being, but not necessarily a living being. I wanted to turn around. I wanted to get in my car, turn around, and drive away.

I knew I was about to enter a palace of pain.

Joanna opened the door to me. A thin, attractive woman in her mid-thirties, she had dark circles under haunted eyes. Small wonder.

She started to lead me through the house.

"If you don't mind," I said, "I'd like to go room to room myself."

"Oh," she replied, a little taken aback. "Please do."

I started my tour, going from room to room. Walking on hardwood floors and beautiful rugs, observing the expensive furniture, the original paintings, and a clerestory ceiling, I had the feeling that I was taking a tour of a museum.

Done downstairs, I climbed the magnificent curved oak stairs to the second floor, went into a master bedroom, then a middle bedroom where pain and sadness hit me like a freight train. I threw my head back, gasping for air, almost screaming for help. I knew that it was in this room that the little boy had taken his life.

Tears welled up in my eyes as I looked around. It was a typical little boy's room, complete and replete with all the things little boys like . . . a baseball bat and glove, posters of ballplayers, and cartoon characters. It was very hard to look at.

God help me, I knew where I had to go. I knew what I had to do.

I walked across the room, the negative energy rocking me almost to the point where I fell down. I opened the closet door. Hot tears spilled down my face. From the intensity of pain I felt I knew this was where Anthony had died. I gradually left my body and was inside him and I saw and felt it all. I saw how empty he was inside. I saw how he took a tie, looped it over the closet pole, and put a paint can inside the closet. I saw how he stood up on the paint can, and how he tied the tie securely around his neck. And I saw a tear come to just one of his eyes.

"Oh, in the name of Jesus *No! No! No! No!*" I screamed. "Don't do it!"

But he did.

He stepped off the paint can and slowly—painfully—choked to death.

It rocked me.

I went down on my knees. I fought for breath. I sobbed uncontrollably.

And then I got control of myself and stood up. I called to Anthony from the other side and he came to me. We talked. Anthony told me that he was doing well. He said that he felt a lot of pain while he was on earth. He had been a little boy climbing a mountain with no summit. He suffered a lot of anguish, a dagger in the heart, more than any child could bear. And although Anthony wished that he had found another way to deal with the pain of his life, although he wished that he had not taken his life, he did say that he was happy now. Free. He was at peace, developing spiritually, getting ready to move on.

Anthony and I talked a lot about why he had taken his life. I understood his actions and he understood that I didn't condone them. He asked me not to talk about the "why" because he doesn't want to cause any more hurt. (That's why I'm not divulging any of the details here, out of respect for Anthony's wishes.) But he did say that if his mommy and daddy wanted to periodically talk to him that he would be happy to do so.

"Please tell my mommy I love her," he said. "Tell her that I'm better now. I'm okay."

Those were the last words I heard from this now peaceful child. I conveyed them to his mother. She smiled and then wept quietly, this time with happiness.

One word frees us of all the weight and pain of life: That word is love.

—Sophocles

I was gratified to leave the house. I was emotionally and physically exhausted and I figured that the farther I got away from the house the more these feelings (physical *and* psychological) would recede. I'd feel better then, I reasoned.

But I didn't.

As I drove home, the negative feelings persisted. No matter what I did to think away the bad thoughts, they just wouldn't leave. And I continued to feel as if I was being strangled.

Well, I thought, maybe they'll go away after a good night's rest. Yes, I told myself. A good night's sleep would be my Rx. That's it. That's all I needed to restore my balance. Only it wasn't. When I awoke the next day—after having been jarred awake a couple of times during the night—I felt the same way I had when I went to bed. It made me a little panicky. What was I going to do?

It was the choking feeling that concerned me the most. Maybe I had something wrong with me physically. Maybe it wasn't anything to do with the case at all, I tried to convince myself. I had a friend who was a doctor and I called him up and told him what my problem was. His office was only a short distance from my house, so I popped in to see him. Normal everything—including an

EKG—declared that I was normal. Healthy. Strong. What was I to do next?

I had a bright idea. I wouldn't do any readings for a week. I would let myself unwind. I would let the pressure go down and let the negative thoughts dissolve.

I did that for seven days and nothing changed.

Again, I didn't know what to do. The pain was too much to endure. Maybe I should quit completely, I thought. Go back to delivering pizza, or maybe manage a McDonald's. But even then there wasn't any guarantee that the pain would go away.

Luckily, I guess, just when I was thinking about a career in fast food, I realized that by stopping the readings I was giving myself a lot more quiet time to focus on the pain. Well, that was no good either. I decided it would be better to keep busy after all. I got back on a regular work schedule, doing individual readings and two to three psychic parties a week. The choking feeling continued, though it didn't get any worse.

Then, something changed—but not for the better. It occurred first with a young woman named Moira who told me through tears that she had been abused by her fraternal grandfather. She was so angry and bitter about this experience that it totally polluted her relationship with men.

I wasn't much help to Moira, at least at the initial appointment, but after the session I found the choking feeling and the sadness and depression engendered by the visit to Anthony going away—only to be replaced by the bitter, cynical, and scared attitude of Moira.

A couple of clients later it happened again. This time a woman wanted to communicate with a baby she had lost. After she left I found myself retaining much of her sadness, plus a little of the cynicism of the woman who had been abused. It was awful.

I didn't know what to do. I got down on my knees and prayed to God. I've always been religious and I've always found that prayer has helped. And it did help a little to release me from these feelings, but just a little. Not as much as I had hoped. The immense pain was still there. I didn't know where to turn.

The things which hurt, instruct.

—Benjamin Franklin

I had known The Aunts for quite awhile by this time, and I was seeing them regularly, but for some reason I never told them about my problem. Maybe I was scared. I mean, if *they* couldn't help me . . . who could?

Then one day a few weeks after the problem started I was at their house and over tea we were having what was to us a very normal conversation about being psychic. The Aunts held me spellbound as they spoke of the way old-time trans-mediums worked. And they scared the living daylights out of me when they showed me how mediums worked by having the dead speak through them. Yes, when you hear a Pavarotti-sized voice issue from the mouth of a delicate eighty-year-old, that's scary.

I was on my third cup of tea by this time. I looked at my watch and it was a little after two. Not that I had to go anywhere right away, but I figured I had taken up enough of The Aunts' time. Or, maybe, I felt I just wanted to get out of there.

"I guess," I said, "I should be going."

They both looked at me.

"But don't you first want to talk about the problem?" Carol asked. "Isn't all this talk just biding time?"

"What problem?" I responded, a little dumbstruck.

"Holding on to the pain of your clients," Helen said.

I was stunned. But why should I have been? I mean they *were* psychics. Two of the best. I hesitated. The Aunts were my final option. If they couldn't help me with my problem, no one could. I let it all go. A Niagara of feeling opened up. I told them all kinds of things, of holding onto the physical and emotional pain of Anthony and the abused woman and the woman who had lost the child and some others besides. Before I knew it my eyes welled over in tears.

Carol reached over and took one of my hands in hers.

"It's all right, Jeffrey," she said, "it's all right."

I cried bitterly, but after five minutes or so, I calmed down. I felt a little better just from having confided in The Aunts. They were wonderful women who really cared, who really could understand what I was going through. Maybe—just maybe—they could help me.

"You're not the first psychic who ever took on the burdens of his clients," Helen said, "and you won't be the last. And you'll do it again, and again . . . all the days of your life. It's a job requirement!"

"The thing is," Carol added chirpily, "there are things you can do to get rid of the pain. Let us teach you how."

"Please," I said, "please."

From that day on they started to teach me techniques for discharging the pain.

DISCHARGING PSYCHIC PAIN

Prayer

"Your impulse to pray is a good one, Jeffrey," The Aunts told me. "Keep it up. You can pray a formal prayer if you like, one of the prayers of your childhood, or you can send a beseeching prayer to the universe asking for assistance in bearing up to the pain. Often prayer isn't so much about asking for circumstances to change as it is about asking for the strength to *bear* the circumstances."

They smiled at each other.

"Some people like to recite the same few lines of a prayer over and over again, while some dwell on just a few words. That's not important. What's important is what works for you. Prayer can provide a beautiful connection with the spiritual world, and that can provide us with strength. It's a call to someone or something outside of ourselves, something larger than ourselves. It's a call for help."

"Funny thing is," they continued "the hurt that results from taking on someone else's psychic pain has a certain goodness

---

Prayer can take us out of ourselves and can provide us with the strength we need to bear psychic pain.

---

about it. The pain you're feeling comes about from your attempts to help other people. And while that may be a difficult thing, it is also a good thing. Try to keep that in mind."

They also suggested that I supplement my prayer with meditation.

"Anything you do to calm yourself is helpful. So relax. Concentrate on your breathing. Make use of the techniques you use to take you to your blue zone. Close your eyes. Trust that you can discharge pain. Trust that peace can be yours."

Music

We spoke about music next, and its tremendous restorative powers. Like prayer, music can take you out of yourself and lead you to a different level of awareness. What's more, music has a wonderful physicality about it. At its simplest level, music can set your feet tapping. But taken to another level, good music can fill your body with promise and can give you an understanding that words just can't capture. So what is good music? Well, that's for you to answer. But I suggest that the music you choose be instrumental only. Lyrics can interfere with the meditative process that cleansing yourself of negativity requires. Remember, the purpose is not to *think*, but to *feel.*

Get comfortable.

Find a place where you won't be disturbed for a while.

Sit in a chair that facilitates good breathing.

Turn off the lights—light a candle if you desire—and simply breathe in the music.

Again, trust is important here. Trust that the music will take you where you need to go. You might feel sad. You might cry. Fine. Be gentle with yourself. Let the music fill your body and ease your sadness away. Know that the psychic pain and negativity you're feeling has come from the universe and that it can be released back into the universe.

Water

Finally, The Aunts taught me about the cleansing power of water.

"By now you understand that it's the simplest properties that will help you clear yourself of negativity," they said. "The profound power of a simple prayer. The strength of a deep breath. The gentle guidance of good music."

Again, they smiled.

"Well, one of the most basic properties of human life is also its strongest. Water."

I looked at them blankly.

"Water is what we use to cleanse our bodies, of course. But water is also what we use to cleanse our spirits."

I paused, then had one of those "lightbulb moments" as I began to grasp the capacity of water for cleansing negativity from the soul. Of course, I was aware of holy water blessings and of the role of water in baptism, which is used symbolically to cleanse original sin. I was even aware of the wonderful healing power of tears. But never had it occurred to me that water could play a part in cleansing the spirit of negativity. I listened intently.

"Go in the shower," The Aunts said, "and set the water at a comfortable temperature. Step under the water and visualize it cleaning your outer body and your inner self too. Use your inner eye to picture the water flowing inside, rinsing away all the negativity and pain. Feel the sorrow run through your body. Take your hands and gently rub them over the areas that are most affected. Close your eyes and feel—really feel—the pain dissipate from your body. If it helps to think of the negativity represented by a particular color, then imagine the water turning that color as the negativity is rinsed from you and down the drain. Imagine this happening, Jeffrey. And it will."

When we cling to pain we end up punishing ourselves.

—Leo F. Buscaglia

Two days later I met with a client who suffered from angina. I felt his tightness and pain very acutely, and also his worry, which was extreme. I decided to give the water a try. I stepped into the shower and let the water run over me. I softly ran my hand over my heart and felt the warm water flowing over the area in a gentle film. I imagined the pain washing away and I felt almost giddy. I really could feel the pain draining away, lessening, calming me. . . . It was almost as if I was being administered an anesthetic. The relief was so palpable that I started to grin uncontrollably. Not only was the pain leaving, but it was being replaced by happiness.

I couldn't believe it. But I should have. I supplemented the water with prayer—for the first time in my life I actually prayed in the shower!—and I stayed under the water for a long time. When I emerged not only the pain of the angina was gone, but also a residue of negativity that I had built up from other readings.

I called The Aunts immediately. They were not surprised when I told them of my success. They would have been surprised if I *hadn't* succeeded! Now they told me how to take the power of water further, to keep water about me during the day to protect me from the negativity that surrounds us all. "After readings," they advised, "when the pain can build up very quickly . . . just wash your hands!" Simple, eh? I took their advice, and now wash my hands and perform the visualization techniques after most sessions. I simply turn on the faucet, and when the water is warm I let it run over my hands, all the while closing my eyes and imaging the negativity running out of me. This "miniature shower" is a highly effective way of performing spiritual cleansing.

Water is a very powerful symbol and can be used to great effect as part of a New Year cleansing ritual. On New Year's Eve, fill a pan with water. Let it sit in your house for several hours, accumulating negativity. Then, when the clock strikes twelve, heralding the New Year, open the front door and discard the water—negativity and all.

There are many ways to incorporate cleansing practices into your day. Some of my clients like to take long baths, while others are soothed by the robust energy of a hot tub! "I imagine," said one client, "that as I sit in the tub and water swirls around it is washing away the negativity and it can't stick to me anymore, inside or out." Of course I don't have a hot tub in my office, but I do have three miniature fountains: two in the waiting room and another on my desk, next to the chair my clients use. The water itself is a very soothing presence, as is the sound.

DEALING WITH GRIEF AND NEGATIVITY

Pain can arise when we hone our psychic abilities to enlarge our spiritual experience. But pain and negativity can also prevent us from making that connection with the spirit world. This was the case with Harold, who came to me for a reading eight years ago. Healthy, handsome, and the successful owner of a haberdashery in Greenwich Village, this forty-year-old man hoped to resolve a long-standing issue related to his mother, Rachel, who had passed. Ten minutes into the session Harold told me that he had something else on his mind, namely that he was uncomfortable in his romantic relationship. Although Harold had a loving and steady partner with whom he had lived for over ten years, he often felt guilty about being gay. "Sometimes," he confided, "I even wish I was straight."

We talked some more and Harold told me that his mother had never fully come to terms with the fact that her son was gay. "She was uncomfortable with my relationship and my sexuality," he said, "and she never really tried to hide it." Harold loved his mother very much, and this lack of acceptance bothered him a great deal. Still, although he missed her and was sad that she had passed, he hoped that now she was at peace he could live peacefully too. Nothing could be further from the truth.

"My mother," he said, "never really accepted me being gay, and she died feeling that way. I thought I could come to terms with her way of thinking, *agree to disagree* as the saying goes, but I can't. I'm very hurt and I want to see this issue resolved. What I was hoping to do was communicate with her. Maybe she's changed her mind. I understand that people can change their minds when they become spirits. I think it could help me get rid of the guilt I feel."

Don't believe that old saw "Time heals all wounds." It doesn't. Not without some effort on your part.

Harold was right about the dead, of course. They arrive on the other side with their personalities intact, but as time goes by they actually grow spiritually, meaning that sometimes they will accept things in the afterlife that they wouldn't accept on earth. But I didn't see this as the total problem in Harold, and my session with him triggered an important insight that was to prove far reaching into my practice.

I told him: "It's too early to try to connect with your mother to resolve this issue. You're in the middle of the grief process, and unless you work through your guilt, which is part of your grief, you won't be able to get closure."

"What do you mean 'grief process'?" Harold asked.

"Well, the grief process is simply the process of coming to terms with a loved one's passing. I shouldn't say 'simply,' though. There's nothing simple about it. It's a complicated process. There's an overwhelming void, a raw grief that settles when you understand that you will never see or speak to a loved one again (in the conventional sense, at least). But it's more than that. The grief process contains a collection of ideas and feelings that occur in response to things that have passed between the two parties. People get entangled in them and they can't move on."

"What kinds of ideas and feelings?"

"The first is denial. Even though a loved one is dead, some people are able to convince themselves that they're not."

"Why . . . ? "

"The death of the person is unbearable. Let me give you an example," I said. "It's actually from a TV drama, but it represents very well what I'm talking about. Years ago I used to watch a cop show called *Police Story.* I remember one episode when a detective and a chaplain come out onto the roof of an apartment building where a middle-aged woman is hanging wash on a line. Very reluctantly, very slowly, but very clearly, the cop and the chaplain tell the woman that it is their sad duty to inform her that her husband, a police officer, has been killed in the line of duty. The woman's response is to thank the cops in a perfunctory way and to continue hanging up the wash. The chaplain and the cop linger a few moments, then the chaplain gives a sign to the cop that that's as far as they are going to get with the woman, and they leave.

"Her heart, you see, could not accept what she had been told, so her mind shut down. It was only later, alone in her kitchen with a cup of coffee that the reality broke through the denial and got to her."

"I understand," Harold said.

"But that's not the end of it," I said. "When denial is released another feeling usually comes up—anger.

Anger is like a thorn in the heart.

—Yiddish proverb

"I'm sure you've seen this in people when their loved ones die. The survivors start howling at the moon, as it were. They get angry at God, angry at fate, angry at a hospital or doctor or whoever. You often hear people say how 'unfair' life is when death occurs.

"Or, they may get mad at the person who died. 'How could you leave me when I need you so much?' is a common refrain."

"It doesn't make a lot of sense," Harold said.

"No," I said, "it doesn't. But it doesn't have to. We're talking about feelings, not logic, and we have to respect our feelings no matter how 'illogical' they appear. Besides, when we're in the grips of our feelings they seem right, the only way. We get fixed on them."

Harold nodded.

"The feeling that interferes most with closure is guilt. Some people may not deny, they may not get angry, but they'll feel guilty."

"How does that work out?"

"In different ways. For example, when someone dies you feel guilty because you tell yourself you didn't do everything you could for the person before they died. Or you didn't treat them well enough during their life. Or maybe you feel you somehow caused their death."

"Caused it?"

"Absolutely. I remember one client who was a very health-conscious person and each day at a certain time she would drive herself and her daughter to a spa where they would work out and then return home.

"One day the woman, a realtor, was too busy to go to the spa, and her daughter drove there alone. Well, on the way to the spa the daughter got involved in a car accident . . . and was killed. Her mother was beside herself with guilt. 'If only I had driven her,' she said. 'If only I had done this, that or the other thing. And why didn't God take me? I've lived a good portion of my life, my daughter hardly lived at all.' People get impaled on guilt, Harold. That's all they think about."

"How about me?"

"Well, I'm a psychic not a shrink, but your guilt, I think, is prompted by the idea that you've somehow failed your mother by being gay. You're all wrapped up in that."

"That's why I want to talk to her one last time."

"No, Harold," I said gently. "Not yet. You're still embroiled in grief, too caught up in your guilt. You're stuck. Making contact with your mother at this stage might cause you a great deal of harm. I would be irresponsible if I helped you."

"But what do I do?" he cried.

"Work it out. Put it behind you. Give yourself time to grieve, to accept your mother's death and to consider your relationship with her. Don't feel guilty. Try to accept yourself without the guilt."

Forgiveness is the key to action and freedom.

—Hannah Arendt

"But how do I do that?"

"It can be a complicated process, but once you work this out you can be at peace with your mother. And that, of course, is the final, healthy phase of the grief process," I explained. "Only when you let go of the guilt can you get to the other side of the grief process."

"But how do you *do* it?" he asked, frustrated.

"In most cases," I added, "people go through the grief process without any outside help. It takes time, but they manage. I think in your case you'd be better off with some help. Seems to me this stuff has been building for a long time."

"So, what are you suggesting?"

"Well, I like to encourage people to look back on their lives and their relationship with their loved ones and to try to thoughtfully examine their time together. In the words of Joan McIntosh, 'Accept the pain, cherish the joys, resolve the regrets.' But that's not always easy to do. You have a lot to untangle, so I suggest a psychologist, perhaps. If you want I can give you a few names."

Harold wasn't thrilled with the idea. In fact, he was bitterly disappointed. He had booked a session with a psychic, after all, and here I was telling him to see a shrink. He wanted magic, but what he really needed was insight. I couldn't give it to him. I could put him in touch with his mother—I could try to act as go-between—but Harold seemed so fragile I knew that it would be the wrong thing to do.

After Harold left that day I thought more about the grief process, and the more I did the more I realized that Harold was not alone in his problem. This was my lightbulb moment. *In many cases people aren't ready to see me. Before I can help them they really need to work through the grief process somewhat, do what they can to put the guilt and anger behind them.* I then began to suggest to clients that they wait at least three months before seeing me after someone has passed. This time varies, of course, but I needed to encourage my clients to take time to work things through so that they could be at least partway on the road to closure. Sometimes I would recommend a professional counselor to talk to—a psychologist, say, or a social worker. And certainly help is available. In addition to private therapists there are many hospitals and organizations that now commonly offer group grief counseling.

In my "post-Harold" world I also came to realize that when it

---

Grief does not end on a schedule, nor will the pain dissipate by an arbitrary designated anniversary.

—Dr. Holly Shaw

---

comes to grief, children shouldn't be forgotten. Indeed, children usually require therapy when a loved one or even a classmate or friend dies. If anyone doubts that, observe how kids act following a death. They're devastated, though they don't tell you that in words. They beam home their mental state in a variety of ways, by acting out their fear and rage, by isolating themselves and going silent, or if they're old enough, by drinking, taking drugs, or engaging in promiscuous behavior. That's the grief process in action, only it's disguised.

The best and most beautiful things in the world cannot be seen or even touched. They must be felt with the heart.

—Helen Keller

About a year after his first visit, Harold returned for a reading, and it was only then that I learned that he had, indeed, followed through on my advice to see someone.

"My guilt over my mother not accepting me was only part of my problem," he told me. "I was putting it all on my mother—it was easy to do because she had passed—but I had other issues with my father and brother that were blindsiding me.

"But now," he said, "we worked those things through."

"That's great," I said, "so why are you here today?"

"I still want to see how my mother feels about me being gay. I still need to know."

"How do you know you're ready to see her?"

"I'm at peace. I've moved on, and I want to know if she has too. I hope she has, I hope that she accepts me, but if she doesn't I'll be okay with it. It would be her problem, not mine. I understand the difference."

I nodded, choked by emotion. Harold had said the magic words: at peace.

I went into my blue zone and asked Rachel to appear. It didn't take long. Almost immediately a beautifully dressed woman in her late sixties appeared, perfectly coiffed, with flawless makeup and sparkling. I didn't need to ask who it was.

"Okay, I said, "right now your mother's standing just a little to the right of you, and she's there with another older female and a male figure. They're watching her. She's telling me that she loves you, she has always loved you, and is very proud of you. If she only knew then, when she was alive, what she learned after she crossed over she would have accepted you and your relationship. She wishes that she could take you in her arms right now. She loves you completely, and wishes you love with your soul mate."

Harold nodded, and when he looked up he was smiling, his eyes misty. Yes, he was at peace.

"Just tell her I love her."

"She knows that."

DÉJÀ VU

- Using your psychic skills can result in spiritual and physical pain, a residue of tapping into the emotions of other people.
- Prayer can help enormously. A beautiful connection to the spiritual world, prayer can provide us with a great deal of strength and resolve. Choose the form and message that work best for you.
- Music has tremendous restorative powers that can help ease psychic pain. Music can take you out of yourself and lead you to a different level of awareness. Just remember that with music therapy the purpose is not to *think,* but to *feel.*
- Water, combined with visualization, can help rinse away negativity. Incorporate water rituals into your daily life. Showers, baths, and fountains all help to combat psychic pain and negativity.
- Sometimes emotional pain can prevent us from getting in touch with the spiritual world. Trust your psychic adviser to help you determine when you're ready to connect with a loved one who has passed. It takes time, and sometimes professional counseling may also be necessary.

ELEVEN

Making the Most of Ghosts

A GHOSTLY APPARITION

About six years ago I got a call from a friend named Scott Trivoli.

"I know this family, the Barons—wife and husband with two boys ten and eleven—who recently moved to Montauk," he said, describing an exclusive area on the east end of Long Island. "They bought this hundred-year-old house at the ocean, and ever since moving in they've been bothered nonstop by all kinds of unexplainable sounds: knocking, whooshing, and tapping. Most of these noises occur in the middle of the night. What's more, they say that about a half dozen times their two boys have seen strange orbs outside the house down near the ocean. They're sure they have ghosts."

"Why?"

"They talked to the Manions, the people who owned the

house before them, and they confirmed that for years they heard the same kinds of sounds and saw the same spotted orbs around the property. The Manions figured they had ghosts, but they actually got used to them."

"What's the problem?" I asked.

"Well, the Barons can't get used to them," Scott said. "They're scared to the point where they're considering selling. Can you help?"

"I'll try."

So, on a clear, moonlit night in late September, I went out to the house to investigate. My psychic instincts instructed me to wait on the porch, which faced the ocean. I scanned the area and listened. Nothing happened for a half hour, then, a tapping noise inside the house. About fifteen minutes after that I spotted an orb moving erratically up and down near the edge of the surf about three feet off the ground. I wasn't sure what I was seeing, but whatever it was, I knew it was restless. I left the porch and walked down to the surf to investigate farther, but I heard no sound, just the hissing of the water as it rolled in and spread out on the sand.

I relaxed myself and tried to make contact.

A minute or so later a dead person appeared. He was old, with mutton chop sideburns and wearing what I took to be a sea captain's clothes: white brimmed cap, blue jacket with brass buttons, blue pants. He seemed very concerned and upset. Self-absorbed. I knew instantly from his demeanor that this was not a regular spirit, but a ghost. I didn't know a great deal about ghosts at the time, but I did know that unlike spirits, ghosts don't return to earth to help people.

Then, a message. Captain Spencer (that was his name) was very upset. More than one hundred years ago he had captained a whaling ship named *The North Star*, until a severe storm had sent both ship and crew to the bottom of the ocean about 400 meters from shore. Captain Spencer was the only survivor. He had not been able to find any of his crew. And he had not been able to rest.

Instantly I knew what the problem was. Even though a great deal of time had passed, Captain Spencer was not aware that he was dead. Well, I wasn't going to be the one to tell him—I didn't know what the implications would be, for one thing—but I was able to suggest, in the nicest way possible, that it would be far better for everyone if he would stop harassing the Barons.

"After all," I said, "you are a Captain of a ship, a person of honor, and you should not be doing this. It reflects badly on you. What's more, you're not honoring the lives of your dead crew."

Captain Spencer looked at me silently for a long time, and then his face relaxed into an expression of agreement. He nodded as his image disappeared. I scanned the ocean, but I could not see him, nor the orb. I hoped that the Barons would never see him again. And they didn't. The captain was a man of his word.

Captain Spencer sparked my interest in ghosts. Since meeting him I have made it my business to find out more. I've even been employed as a sort of "ghost buster" by some people who were being harassed. Learning about ghosts is vital to developing your psychic skills. Knowledge of ghosts will increase your overall

---

Vision is the art of seeing things invisible.

—Jonathan Swift

---

knowledge of the spiritual world and will help you hone your psychic abilities so that, if you ever meet a ghost, you won't be afraid. Or quite so afraid anyway.

THE SPIRITUAL UNIVERSE

In the first place, from what I've seen, ghosts are just another type of spirit, with one important exception: They come from a different place, literally and figuratively. We all know that just as there is a physical world, there is a spiritual universe too. Well, that spiritual universe contains a number of levels, countries if you will.

The Heaven World

The best country is Heaven, or the Heavenworld. Members of most major religious groups strive to get into this Heavenworld. No surprise there. As I see it, Heaven is where God resides, a place where souls live in perpetual peace, harmony, and happiness with none of the cares of our earth-bound world. What does it look like? I don't know. I've never seen it, nor have I spoken to anyone who has. But I do know that Heaven is a consciousness and I suspect it might mean different things to different people. For some it may be a very familiar setting—something well-known or well loved—while for others it may be a utopian existence, a place where their deepest desires are at last fulfilled. Different reports of Heaven abound, and I don't want to confirm or contradict any of them. What I do know, however, is that it's important for me to admit the limitations of my knowledge and experience, and also to be open to the possibilities that surround us—Heaven included.

The Spirit World

The next best country I call the Spirit World, a sort of pre-Heaven, a place where souls congregate while waiting to enter the Heavenworld. Certain souls wait in the Spirit World because they are not quite in the state of perfect spiritual goodness that Heaven requires. These souls are good, but not quite good enough, so they go to the Spirit World to develop their goodness prior to entering Heaven. I don't know all the things that contribute to this perfect goodness, but I do know that prayer helps greatly. This prayer can come from the spirits themselves, and it can also be made on their behalf by people remaining on earth.

Again, I wish I could tell you what the Spirit World looks like, but I can't. I do know, however—from my own experience in the psychomanteum and from speaking with people who have passed over and returned—that a portion of the Spirit World is comprised of a dark tunnel that gets brighter as you walk down it and that terminates in a very bright light. Personally, I believe that this very bright light is the door to Heaven. Hence, the phrase "Going to the light" means heading for Heaven.

It is this Spirit World that houses the souls who come to help the living. Remember: Souls who inhabit this world are essentially good. They return to Earth in various forms to help us. Whether they are called or whether they sense they are needed, they return to Earth out of love for those who have remained behind. Doing these good deeds, I suspect, also helps them speed their entry into Heaven.

The Astral Plane

Technically speaking, ghosts *are* spirits, but they are low man on the spiritual totem pole so to speak. Ghosts live in the Astral

Plane, an immense dark flat field, with a dim light that is crowded with millions of souls in human form. These souls, dressed in the clothes in which they died or were buried—street clothes, really—mill around aimlessly with little joy or hope. The Astral Plane is mostly a place of sadness and depression.

But not for all.

Many ghosts have hope. Many ghosts know that they can develop themselves to a state where they can enter first the Spirit World, and later Heaven.

Ghosts on the Astral Plane are not all there for the same reasons. Some, for example, are people who have died and are not even aware of it, like Captain Spencer. This segment of the ghostly population comprises souls who have lost their lives violently—say in an accident, a war, or through murder. These ghosts were living their lives when suddenly . . . they were terminated. Gone. Like traveling on a train that abruptly enters a tunnel. All of a sudden, darkness.

There are exceptions. While most people who die precipitously end up on the Astral Plane as ghosts, not everyone does. Children, I believe, go directly to the Spirit World or Heaven and so do cops, firemen, and others who have dangerous and noble occupations. Children are pure innocent beings. And certain adults have been doing good things, perfecting their souls, praying and, in a sense, readying themselves for death by their good works. When they die, they're not caught by surprise, their souls undeveloped. They're ready to go.

Some ghosts are stuck on the Astral Plane because they don't believe in God. Atheists in life, they are also atheists in death. For those who don't believe, there is no process to meet God. There is no Heaven. Other ghosts are on the Astral Plane because they are afraid of God. They don't want to take any steps to stand in judg-

After death we are not disembodied spirits. Somewhere in God's wonderful creation there is a place where we can again be with those we have loved and lost for a while.

—C. L. Allen

ment before God because they know that they have lived evil lives and will be banished to Hell or its equivalent. Better to wander around with nowhere than to face that, they may think.

The last variety of ghosts includes those who simply have not developed spiritually, or who have led meaningless, immoral, or possibly evil lives. Where do you think that people like Hitler and Vlad the Impaler go? That's right. The Astral Plane.

The range of spiritual development of ghosts differs greatly, which translates into different rates of entering the Spirit World. Some move relatively quickly—it may take them just days or weeks—while others take a longer time, which may be months, years, or even hundreds of years. Still, no matter what type of life you've lived on earth, you *can* get to Heaven.

Prayer helps souls in the Spirit World get to Heaven. Prayer also helps ghosts develop so that they can leave the Astral Plane for the Spirit World. Ghosts can pray for themselves, and so can living people. It may seem incomprehensible to pray for some of the monsters of history, but prayer is one of the things it takes for them to move on. And you know what? There are many souls now living on earth who have the capacity and the love in their hearts to do this. I'm sure you've seen on TV, for example, where mothers or other family members will come forward to save the life of someone who has murdered a daughter, a son, a spouse, etc. These are the kinds of people—great souls—who can pray for the likes of a Hitler or Stalin.

UNDERSTANDING GHOSTS

Now to the big question: Why do ghosts haunt us? What do they expect to accomplish? I think many ghosts dislike themselves. They feel angry and want to unload that anger onto someone else. And guess who that turns out to be? Earthbound souls. You and me. A ghostly appearance is actually an angry outburst. The ghost is angry and wants to scare us.

Ghosts have their own criteria for selecting the places or people they choose to harass. I suspect that, in general, they look for like-minded living people. For example, if a house has an alcoholic in it, and the ghost is an alcoholic, that's who he'll choose to

---

In my visions of this Astral Plane I think of ghosts as having a clear view of Earth, including everyone and everything on it.

---

haunt. If someone is addicted to drugs, the ghost or ghosts will invade that home. If the ghost was a murderer in life, she will likely seek out a murderer. Certain people are perfect targets for a ghost's hostility.

Why so focused? Probably because of self-loathing. In a sense, many ghosts haunt in order to attack themselves—the persona they don't like.

But not all ghosts are motivated this way. Some, like the sea captain, have a generalized anger and are just looking for someone to take it out on. And of course, in the sea captain's case, proximity was important. He chose to haunt the site that was causing him great pain, the place where his ship went down. Ghosts will often haunt a place instead of a person—the famous old haunted-house stories, for example—that they believe are the site of their pain and anger.

Not all ghosts are angry, though. Some are lonely souls just stuck on the Astral Plane, developing, but not that quickly. It can be lonely waiting to develop, that's why a ghost will take up residence in a cemetery, or again, in a house where he once lived. These ghosts don't mean to scare us, even though they do.

The main problem in dealing with ghosts is that when you're first starting out it's hard to tell the difference between a ghost and spirit, that is, an inhabitant of the Astral Plane and one from the Spirit World. After all, ghosts and spirits come in the same physical forms: mists, orbs, full human form, and flashes, etc. So how do you know the difference? You will be able to tell the difference as you begin to develop your psychic skills, much like a diamond merchant can tell the real diamond from the false stone. But in the beginning, the best way to distinguish between ghosts and spirits is by doing a "spiritual profile" on them.

The important thing for the budding psychic to realize is that ghosts cannot hurt you physically, although they can cause you emotional damage if you let them. You can get ghosts to leave if you wish, usually just by talking nicely to them. Sometimes yelling works, though. Ironically, ghosts scare easily.

- Does the being seem to take pleasure in playing with psychic energy?
- Does it make noises or unexpected appearances that don't seem to have any purpose except scaring you?
- Does the being seem to have no interest in helping you?
- Does the being seem intent on giving you direct answers that turn out to be wrong?
- Does it want to play, but in a cruel and mischievious manner?
- And finally, do your instincts tell you that this being is a ghost?

If the answer to most of these questions is yes, then chances are the being is a ghost. Remember: Spirits have a goal to help you in some way. Ghosts don't. That's the main difference.

PHOTOGRAPHING GHOSTS

Photographing ghosts is a good way to sharpen your psychic skills and enhance your awareness of the spiritual universe. We deal with a different dimension when we deal with ghosts, and for some reason this dimension is seen more easily in pictures than with the naked eye. Ghosts are caught between two worlds on the Astral Plane, and the quick shutter speed of a camera is perfect for capturing that world.

It's exhilarating to capture ghosts on camera. Imagine: physical evidence of the spirit world!

Here are some lessons I learned from my computer guru Jim DeCaro who has photographed ghosts extensively—he even took the picture for the cover of this book!

Before attempting to photograph or record a ghost, you should prepare yourself adequately. Remember: This is probably going to be a scary experience. (Jim is an ex-Marine, not a shrinking violet, and even he said the experience scared the hell out of him!) There isn't any way to totally eliminate your fear, but it should help to remember that ghosts are not evil, merely troublesome. Hollywood has portrayed ghosts as monsters, but they're not that way at all.

Don't go into the situation with an adversarial attitude. This may set up a reciprocal attitude on the part of the ghosts. I knew one really macho guy, David, who said he refused "to be cowed" by the ghosts he was going to photograph in an old cemetery nearby in New Hampshire. So one pitch-black early morning he strode boldly into the cemetery, camera in hand, and said very loudly, "You bastards don't scare me," and then proceeded to do the shoot.

About fifteen minutes into the shoot this macho man started to get a creepy feeling. Sensing something was behind him, he turned and saw a huge cloud of mist, in the center of which he saw eyes and a mouth. As if that weren't bad enough, he heard a large and threatening sigh emit from this "thing." David didn't look so macho running out of the cemetery as fast as his legs could carry him!

Be as friendly as possible. Start up a conversation that asks, out loud, how the ghosts are doing. Admit that you're afraid and ask for help in not being afraid. Tell the ghosts who you are (although they already know), and offer them some tangible gifts, something you think they may like. In Jim's case, he had carried out extensive research on the area in which he lived and had learned that hundreds of years earlier his neighborhood had actually been home to many Indians. So, before he started shooting, he set out some tobacco, which they highly regarded.

There is no great mystery to photographing ghosts, nor is there a formula or psychic recipe. Just this: Use your instincts and be respectful. There isn't a special place to photograph ghosts either (they live just about everywhere, in houses, in backyards, in cemeteries, and elsewhere); nevertheless, cemeteries are good places to start, simply because they're likely to be bustling with ghosts who are lonely for the companionship of other ghosts.

I often suggest to people that they start off with a flash Polaroid. Trust me when I say that some people will doubt that you have obtained pictures of actual ghosts. These suspicious minds believe that you doctored the film during development. But Polaroids are impregnable. They can't be doctored.

Though I do believe that almost anyone can fine up their psychic abilities and make contact with the other side, I've long known that Jim DeCaro possesses the high level of sensitivity especially suited to photographing ghosts. Indeed, I had been bugging Jim to "get to work" for months before he actually did. Toting his new megapixel digital camera (Jim didn't care about the skeptics), he went alone into a local "haunted" cemetery near his home.

"I just stood among the headstones," Jim said, "and let my instincts guide me. I tried hard *not* to try hard, if that makes any sense. I just followed my impulses and started taking some random shots, two dozen in all."

Jim didn't really expect any ghosts to appear on the film. Certainly there was no hint of them as he was clicking off the pictures. In fact, the scene was very ordinary: just a crisp, clear night, a maroon sky threatening rain the next day, and headstones—some black silhouettes, others pale with moonlight. But, as he was to tell me later:

"I began to scroll through the pictures, not seeing anything unusual until, around the ninth or tenth picture, I saw something that made my heart jump and my stomach go hollow. There was a glowing, three-dimensional circular object around two or three feet above one of the headstones. I'm sure I hadn't seen it there when I took the picture. I was overwhelmed. Well, I quickly scrolled through the remaining pictures—and found several more."

These orbs were small, so in order to see them better Jim fed the film into his computer, which has dual 21-inch monitors. He froze. "I was dumbfounded," he said. "Six of these pictures contained the same bright glowing objects. I knew they were ghosts but I didn't know much else."

Jim brought the pictures to me for interpretation. We analyzed the photos together, and I was able to confirm that the pictures were indeed of ghosts. Specifically, the spirits appeared to be energy clusters of children who were playing in the cemetery.

This really got Jim's attention. The day I gave him my interpretation (and confirmed his own reluctant suspicions), he actually returned to the cemetery and, using the headstones in the photos as a guide, looked for the exact spots where he had taken the shots. Sure enough, he found them. "I began reading markings on the stones and within a twenty-foot radius found no less than six children under the age of ten."

He was excited, but sad, too. "My excitement," he said, "gave way to an odd feeling of sadness when the reality hit me. These are the spirits of children. And here they are."

On his second trip to the cemetery Jim was interrupted by the local police and told he couldn't shoot there. So, he regrouped, as it were, and walked along outside the cemetery, shooting through the fence as he did. He took about fifty shots, and immediately noticed that these images were different. "There were many objects in each picture," he said, "that I couldn't see through the viewfinder in the camera . . . misty smoke . . . streams of light . . . and then a very bright white mist of smoke that first appeared in one picture and then took me by surprise by appearing in another. After using all my film I felt all shook up because I had a sense that what I saw also saw me."

As I mentioned, you don't have to photograph ghosts in a cemetery. Just about any place will do. Jim didn't want to be hassled by the police so he decided to try his next photo shoot closer to home.

Millions of spiritual creatures walk the earth, both when we sleep and when we wake.

—John Milton

"Sometime after week four or five," he told me, "I went into my backyard and started snapping away." And he was primed to do so because, as you have learned by now, the more psychic things you do, the more you become attuned and the more receptive the spirits become to your efforts. They like the attention.

Jim developed a regimen. Every night, after laying out tobacco, he would shoot for twenty minutes, coming up with about fifty or sixty pictures. Then the results really started to come in.

"By week seven I began getting human shapes in mist," Jim said. "Smiling and unsmiling faces, sometimes with an amazing amount of detail. Also shapes of bodies, animals, some very large, small animals, sometimes skeletal figures." He also got streaks of light: three-dimensional orbs, colored orbs . . . all those forms of energy in which souls appear. His best shot occurred almost by chance.

"I had already taken fifty or so pictures," he told me, "and decided to stop and just listen. So I stood there for five minutes, I guess, when I got the urge to take one last shot. It happened in a millisecond.

"As I held the camera up to my chest and snapped, I saw a man standing in front of me. We met at eye level and he was standing so close to me—no more than a foot or so—that I jumped back. For that millisecond he was fully solid, man size, bright white, and looking straight at me. Right into my heart. And then, he was gone.

"Heart racing, I ran into the house to see if I had captured the man on film."

Jim showed the picture to me. It was an amazing shot, clearly the photo of a North American Indian with a wolf by his side. I knew right away why he was there: He was not a ghost, but Jim's spirit guide, just as I had my Indian spirit guide. The Indian was no doubt there to make sure Jim was okay. Jim basked in it all, because from that moment on he felt an amazing sense of protection.

As I mentioned, ghosts "haunt" houses and it is not unusual to find them in and around homes—ghosts can become attached to a house for hundreds of years and at one point in his photo taking Jim told me that they started showing up, making themselves known, inside his house. "I would hear doors opening and closing, or tapping, or someone trying to get in as well as other eerie sounds."

In some cases, you may encounter some ghosts which make you feel down. If you want to get rid of this, you can use the tips and hints contained in "Cleansing Yourself of Negativity." You can also insure that ghosts don't get into the house by burning sage at each of the windows and doors once a day. I earlier mentioned that if you want to drive ghosts out just yell at them to get the heck out!

Photographing ghosts is more than a neat party trick. It teaches you to see with your instincts rather than your eyes. It teaches you to trust. What's more, photographing ghosts will help you to be aware of that other dimension we call the Astral Plane, and to respect those who are still pursuing their greatest spiritual development. So, to begin:

The expert at anything was once a beginner.

—Abby Hayes

- Don't perform spirit photography in a group—it's not a group exercise. Though you can obtain results with numerous persons on site during a shooting session, I believe the individual should exercise restraint from doing so. Spirits can feel the vibrations of those people involved and you would not want to be held accountable for the intentions of someone other than yourself.
- Spirit photography should be a natural occurrence. Although certain rituals can be used to conjure spirits, there is a certain satisfaction and fulfillment gained from a natural approach. For me, my religious background plays a part in my decision not to conjure. On the other hand, a totally natural approach is something that has been given and not taken. This addresses my moral concerns to any form of spirit communication.
- Try to bring more than one camera. If you start getting activity, you'll need to shoot quickly because spirits move very fast.
- Save the negatives or digital film cartridges. If you happen to capture some amazingly incredible shots, you

may someday need to produce the originals for authentication. Better to have than to have not.

- Make every effort to ensure that no other common anomaly is impairing your shot.
- Behave in a respectful manner and do not attempt to dare, provoke, or intimidate a spirit. Your intentions will be felt by the spirit and returned accordingly.

DÉJÀ VU

- The spiritual universe consists of three worlds: the Heavenworld, the Spirit World, and the Astral Plane.
- Heaven is where God resides, a place where souls live in perpetual peace, harmony, and happiness. The Spirit World is sort of pre-Heaven where souls congregate while waiting to enter the Heavenworld. The Astral Plan is where ghosts reside. They need to develop themselves to a state where they can enter first the Spirit World, and later Heaven.
- Ghosts are just another type of spirit. But unlike spirits, ghosts don't feel the need to help those on earth. Ghosts may be scary, but they can't harm us physically.
- Prayer helps ghosts move from the Astral Plane to the Spirit World. It also helps spirits ascend to Heaven.
- The camera can see ghosts that the human eye may not see. Shoot them at night, starting with a Polaroid camera with flash. Don't try to "see" the ghosts, just relax and let your instincts guide you. Then start shooting!

TWELVE

Practice Makes Psychic

YOUR TURN

I believe psychic ability is inborn, that everyone has it to varying degrees, and that there actually exists a physical mechanism that sends and receives psychic energy. This wonderful and mysterious mechanism is located in that vast unexplored part of our brain, and it translates psychic information into messages that can be understood by our own sixth sense. The more we develop our psychic abilities, the more efficient our sixth sense becomes.

I make my living as a psychic intuitive. You don't have to. You probably don't want to. But if you've read this book chances are you want to discover your own psychic abilities and harness them for your own good, and the good of those around you. You can.

What's the best way to take your skills to that next level? Focus on your attitude. Develop a psychic mind-set toward life. Doubt so-called coincidences. Look below—and above!—the surface. Question the obvious. Learn to read auras. Tap into conscious and unconscious happenings. Pay attention to your dreams and be faithful in keeping a dream journal.

Be willing to believe.

Your success in harnessing your psychic abilities will depend on the approach you take, so put your logical, questioning mind on hold and think about the world psychically. Be aware of how you react to the world. Try to put those logical explanations on hold. Unhook your mind from the restrictions of so-called logic and reason and be willing to accept the influences of the world that you can't see. Look at the world with the eyes of a psychic.

THE GAMES PSYCHICS PLAY

Have fun with it. Play psychic games to get your energy flowing. Practice psychometry. Exercise your visualization skills. Take time each day to meditate. Let your mind wander. Amuse yourself with the questions "what if" and "I wonder." Go on a hunch. Listen to your gut. Guess. Suppose. Presume. Be open. Think for a moment before saying "no." Dismantle your defenses. Look at the world through the eyes of a child. What have you got to lose?

DOING TIME

If you really want to harness your psychic abilities, it's a good idea to devise a training schedule, just as you would if you were trying to perfect any other skill. Ultimately how far and how fast you progress will depend on your own individual abilities, but if you give yourself some psychic homework and are faithful to your schedule, then chances are you should start seeing results in a few short weeks.

Meditate

Frequency: Twice a week, or more.
Duration: Twenty minutes, or as needed.
Task: Unhook the phone. Find a quiet comfortable space. Devote yourself to calming your mind, ridding yourself of the stresses and responsibilities of your wordly life, and prepare to open yourself to the limitless possibilities of the other world.

Analyze Your Dreams

Frequency: Every night.
Duration: N/A
Task: Upon waking, take a few minutes to jot down the salient points of your dreams. Consider the nature of your dreams and ask yourself whether they were psychic in nature or not. Once a month look back through your dream journal and see if you can

make any psychic connections that may not have been apparent when the dream took place.

Cleanse Yourself of Negativity

Frequency: As needed.
Duration: Thirty minutes to an hour, or as desired.
Task: Pray. Ask for assistance from a higher power and from those who love you in the spirit world. Employ water-cleansing rituals, light candles, and play soothing music.

Visualize

Frequency: Every other day at first, then daily.
Duration: Thirty-five minutes at first, then intermittently throughout the day.
Task: Get the "psychic juices" going. Use visualization techniques to enhance your psychic ability, to discharge negativity, and to help you achieve your goals.

Practice Psychometry

Frequency: Once or twice a week.
Duration: N/A
Task: Take a small object belonging to someone else. Relax. Try to receive the energies of the object, and then to understand it. You'll get better at this with practice.

Contact the Dead

Frequency: Every other day.
Duration: Thirty minutes to an hour.

Task: Get yourself into your blue zone or put a possession of the deceased under your pillow. Relax. Let your mind reach toward the Spirit World, but don't force it. Be gentle with yourself. Let your mind take you where you need to go. Be open to the possibilities of contact, either while you're awake or via your dreams.

Test Yourself

Frequency: Daily.
Duration: N/A
Task: Write down a series of questions for yourself when you get up in the morning. Answer them using your intuition and psychic ability. Keep track. See how you improve over time.

Photograph Spirits

Frequency: Once a month, or less.
Duration: N/A
Task: Take a Polaroid flash camera to a graveyard after dusk. Don't focus, but let your instincts guide you and . . . click, click, click.

Set Your Psychic Mind-set

Frequency: Every day.
Duration: N/A
Task: Approach the world with your psychic side active. Focus on revaluating the psychic character of your everyday happenings. Look beyond the surface of events and trust your instincts. If you think it was a psychic occurrence, chances are, it was.

Keep a Journal

Frequency: Every day.
Duration: N/A
Task: Jot down psychic events during the day. Did you follow your instinct to a parking place, for example? Did you experience an unusual number of "coincidences?" Did you *know* something was going to happen and were proved right? Record the psychic happenings in your life—the successful ones and the unsuccessful ones. Notice patterns. Acknowledge your feelings. Look back on your journal regularly. Chances are it will provide information on the areas you need to work on.

Glossary

ASTRAL PLANE. The place where ghosts reside, the astral plane is an immense surface with very little light, located below Heaven and the Spirit World.

AURA. The light that emanates from a person's physical body, an aura represents the reflection of our spiritual essence, and as such, can provide us with a physical and spiritual profile. Auras are manifest in different colors, each color signifying a particular state of being.

CLOSURE. A satisfactory resolution to a painful issue with a loved one following death, closure may include saying good-bye, releasing guilt, expressing feelings, or determining the well-being of someone who has crossed over.

CONSCIOUS INFLUENCE. Psychic energy that yields information we're consciously aware of, such as intuition and extrasensory perception. (See also "Psychic Perceptions, Conscious.")

CROSSED OVER. The term commonly used in the psychic world to indicate a death or passing, crossing over implies that the action of dying is not the end of life, but simply the crossing from this world to the next.

ENERGY FORMS. The different ways in which the dead appear, such as full body, lights, neon, mists, and orbs. Form follows energy; it's the energy that gives life to the form.

GHOST. The spirit of a dead person not spiritually developed, a ghost is considered "low man on the spiritual totem pole." Ghosts can develop spiritually through prayer, though, and it's important to remember that while they may be troublesome, they cannot harm you.

HEAVENWORLD. The place beyond the light where souls at peace live for eternity, the Heavenworld (often called just "Heaven") accepts souls of all backgrounds and religions, the only qualification being that the soul is at rest.

LIGHT. The bright, warm light that appears to those who are crossing over after death. Those who have had near-death experiences describe a tunnel of light which leads to the brightest light of all and describe the experience as overwhelmingly positive.

MEDITATION. The mental process that leads to a calm mind, a "psychic zone" that allows the reception of energy and spirits.

MEDIUM. A psychic "middleman" who facilitates communication between the dead and the living.

NEAR-DEATH EXPERIENCE. The term coined by Dr. Raymond Moody in his book *Life After Life,* a near-death experience or NDE occurs when someone who is clinically dead comes back to life. Those who have experienced an NDE describe floating above their bodies watching as doctors work to bring them back to life. They also consistently describe the presence of a warm light.

PSYCHIC. The ability to read and transmit energies, the sixth sense. Everyone is psychic to varying degrees, but in most the potential for psychic ability is undeveloped.

PSYCHIC DREAM. Vivid or containing unusual colors, psychic dreams often have a special impact on the dreamer. (Dreams have the potential to tap into an amazing amount of psychic energy, but not all dreams are psychic.)

PSYCHIC PERCEPTIONS, CONSCIOUS. The intuition or ESP that alerts us to something which we have no logical way of knowing. Conscious psychic perceptions give us a sense of people, places, or situations, often revealing danger or emotion that is not readily apparent. (See also "Conscious Influence")

PSYCHIC PERCEPTIONS, UNCONSCIOUS. An insight of which we are not consciously aware, yet causes us to act in an unusual way. An unconscious psychic perception can only be recognized after it has occurred. (See also "Unconscious Influence")

PSYCHOMANTEUM (ORACLE OF THE DEAD). Originally built by the ancient Greeks, the psychomanteum is a room where people mirror gaze in hopes of seeing loved ones who have crossed over.

PSYCHOMETRY. The practice of reading a person's energy by touching a personal possession.

READING. A one-on-one session in which a psychic provides information or advice to a client.

SIGNS. Little indicators the dead leave to show us that they're still around. Signs may include mundane objects such as feathers or pennies, smells, sounds, or changes in temperature.

SOUL ENERGY. All human beings (living or dead) give off energy, as do places and inanimate objects. This soul energy contains information about the past, present, and future, and is transmitted back and forth between the living and the living, and the living and the dead.

SPIRIT PHOTOGRAPHY. Photography of beings that are commonly believed to be invisible. Spirit photography captures the energy of the spirit in a concrete image.

SPIRIT WORLD. The place where spirits wait prior to entering Heaven, also called "pre-Heaven."

UNCONSCIOUS INFLUENCE. The unconscious flow of psychic energy that motivates us to do something—without our awareness. (See also "Psychic Perception, Unconscious")

VISUALIZATION. The act of conjuring pictures in the mind, visualization makes use of an orchestrated, sustained—deliberately focused—effort to recall and create images.